Roadmap
to the
Virginia SOL
EOC Virginia and
United States History

The Princeton Review
educators.princetonreview.com

Roadmap
to the Virginia SOL
EOC Virginia and United States History

by
Laura
Schaefer

Random House, Inc.
New York

www.randomhouse.com/princetonreview

This workbook was written by The Princeton Review, one of the nation's leaders in test preparation. The Princeton Review helps millions of students every year prepare for standardized assessments of all kinds. The Princeton Review offers the best way to help students excel on standardized tests. The Princeton Review is not affiliated with Princeton University or Educational Testing Service.

Princeton Review Publishing, L.L.C.

160 Varick Street, 12th Floor

New York, NY 10013

E-mail: textbook@review.com

Published in the United States by Random House, Inc., New York.

ISBN 0-375-76438-0

Series Editor: Russell Kahn

Content Editor: Michael Bagnulo

Design Director: Tina McMaster

Art Director: Neil McMahon

Production Editor: Kimberly Craskey

Production Coordinator: Robert Kurilla

Manufactured in the United States of America

9 8 7 6 5 4 3 2 1

First Edition

CONTENTS

ACKNOWLEDGMENTS

To my mom, Linda Hintze Artz, and my dad, Michael Schaefer, for always encouraging me to ask questions and seek answers.

INTRODUCTION

ABOUT THIS BOOK

Roadmap to the Virginia Standards of Learning Assessments: End of Course Virginia and United States History is designed to help you prepare for the Standards of Learning (SOL) assessment in Virginia and U.S. history in two ways:

- by reinforcing your understanding of Virginia and U.S. history and by promoting the development of skills outlined in the Virginia Standards of Learning
- by providing you with lots of practice questions that are similar to the questions you will have to answer on the actual test

This book has three parts: history review, lessons, and practice tests. The history review includes information on important people, places, and events in Virginia and U.S. history. The lessons provide practice questions that will help you develop the skills you will need to do well on the test. The practice tests give you the opportunity to try out your refreshed understanding in a format similar to the actual SOL assessment.

Before you make your way through this book, take a look at the table of contents and skim through the pages to get an idea of what to expect. You might discover that you feel more comfortable with some concepts and skills than others. We recommend that you do *all* the lessons, but if you don't have enough time, focus your attention on the lessons that cover concepts and skills that are new or difficult for you.

A description of each of the sections of the book follows.

THE BIG PICTURE

The SOL assessment in Virginia and U.S. history tests your understanding of the people, places, and events that you learned about in your Virginia and U.S. history course. This section reviews much of the content that is likely to be tested by the End of Course exam. It is not a replacement for your history textbook, but it does include some key points for easy reference.

LESSONS

The SOL assessment in Virginia and U.S. history includes multiple-choice items, which offer four answer choices from which you select the correct answer. All of the lessons in this book provide you with approaches for answering multiple-choice items. You can use these approaches to answer questions on the practice tests and on the actual SOL assessment.

Each of the seventeen lessons in this book addresses one or more of the standards outlined in the Virginia Standards of Learning for Virginia and U.S. history. The SOL assessment in Virginia and U.S. history is designed to test your grasp of the concepts and skills included in these standards. The standard or standards that each lesson reviews are quoted at the beginning of the lesson. Each lesson includes

- *What this means:* An explanation of the standard and the kinds of questions that may be asked on the test to assess your understanding of the standard
- *Sample:* A sample multiple-choice item
- *How to Answer:* A step-by-step demonstration of how to answer the sample question using test-taking strategies
- *Tips:* These tips will give you pointers on the SOL assessment, history concepts and skills, and test-taking in general
- *Now You Try It!:* Practice questions for you to answer on your own

REVIEWS
This book includes four cumulative review sections to give you more practice. Each review section covers the concepts and skills addressed in the lessons that precede it.

ANSWER KEY FOR THE LESSONS AND REVIEWS
You can check your answers to all questions in the *Now You Try It!* sections of the lessons and in the review sections in the answer key that begins on page 165. The answer key provides the correct answer to each question. *Do not read the answers before you try the questions yourself.* It is better to try your best on your own and then compare your work with the answers afterward.

THE PRACTICE TESTS
After the lessons and review sections, there are two full-length practice tests that give you a chance to take your refreshed understanding of Virginia and U.S. history for a test drive. Each practice test is similar in structure and content to an actual SOL assessment in Virginia and U.S. history. The instructions for taking the practice tests are on page 174. Read the instructions completely before you take the tests.

ANSWERS AND EXPLANATIONS FOR THE PRACTICE TESTS
You can check your answers to all practice test questions in the answers and explanations section that begins on page 211. In addition to correct answers, this section provides explanations of why the answers are correct or incorrect.

ABOUT THE STANDARDS OF LEARNING ASSESSMENT IN VIRGINIA AND U.S. HISTORY

WHAT IS THE PURPOSE OF THE SOL ASSESSMENT IN VIRGINIA AND U.S. HISTORY?

The SOL assessment in Virginia and U.S. history is used to show that Virginia public high school students who are completing a course in Virginia and U.S. history have mastered the concepts and skills that the state has determined are essential. Passing the SOL assessment in Virginia and U.S. history may earn you one of the verified credits that you need in order to receive a diploma.

Virginia public high school students need a minimum of six verified credits in order to graduate with a Standard Diploma. For students who entered the ninth grade in the 2003–2004 school year, one of these verified credits must be earned by passing an SOL exam in history and social science. (For an Advanced Studies Diploma, you need nine verified credits, two of which must be earned in history and social science courses.) In order to earn a verified credit, you must take pass an SOL course and the associated SOL exam.

Even if you have already earned the verified credits that you need for your diploma, you must take the SOL test for any course you are taking that is associated with an SOL test. The results of the test help the state decide whether or not your school is doing its job to educate you. Furthermore, your school may incorporate your performance on an SOL test into your final grade for the related course.

CAN I TAKE THE SOL ASSESSMENT IN VIRGINIA AND U.S. HISTORY AGAIN IF I DO NOT PASS?

Yes. In order to earn a verified credit for your diploma, you can retake the test until you pass it.

WHEN IS THE SOL ASSESSMENT IN VIRGINIA AND U.S. HISTORY ADMINISTERED?

The SOL assessment in Virginia and U.S. history is administered in the spring semester of the year that you take your Virginia and U.S. history course. SOL assessments are also administered in the summer and fall to students who need to retake any tests.

WHAT'S ON THE SOL ASSESSMENT IN VIRGINIA AND U.S. HISTORY?

The SOL assessment in Virginia and U.S. history tests how well you understand the concepts and skills outlined in the Virginia Standards of Learning for Virginia and U.S. history. The concepts and skills you have been learning in your history class are also based on these standards.

How Is the SOL Assessment in Virginia and U.S. History Structured?

- The SOL assessment in Virginia and U.S. history includes 70 multiple-choice items. Of those items, only 60 are scored. The other 10 items are Field Test Items that the state is trying out for later administrations of the test. You will not know which items are being field-tested, so answer every question as though it counts.

- Each multiple-choice item offers four answer choices from which you select the correct answer. You record your answers to multiple-choice items by filling in bubbles on an answer sheet.

How Do I Approach the Test?

- Pace yourself. When you sit down to take the test, take a deep breath, relax, and focus. The SOL assessment in Virginia and U.S. history is not timed, so there is no need to rush through questions. If you work too quickly, you are more likely to make careless mistakes. Instead, pace yourself by working carefully through each question. When you come to a question you can't answer, don't get stuck and waste valuable time. Skip it and come back to answer it later. It's better to move on to other questions that you might find easier.

- Take your best guess. When you reach the end of the test, there will probably be some questions that you had to skip. Make sure you go back and answer every question before handing in your test! Any question left blank will be marked wrong, so it's better to take your best guess and maybe get the question correct than to leave it blank and guarantee that you'll get it incorrect.

- Check your work. If you finish the test with time to spare, use the extra time to review your answers. You don't get any extra points for finishing early, so it's better to double-check as many of your answers as you can. Make sure you didn't make any silly mistakes, like filling in the wrong answer bubble!

- Be comfortable. It's important to feel rested and comfortable on the testing day in order to do your best. Try to get plenty of sleep for several nights before the test. Make sure to eat well on the day you take the test. Be prepared: Bring several pencils, a sharpener, a calculator, a ruler, a watch, and tissues (if you need them). Use the bathroom just before test time.

ANSWERING MULTIPLE-CHOICE QUESTIONS

The SOL assessment in Virginia and U.S. history is comprised of multiple-choice questions. The following four practices are key to answering these questions correctly:

- *Always* examine any chart, graph, map, or illustration that accompanies a question on the test.
- *Always* read *every* answer choice—even if you think that the first choice is correct.
- Use key words in the question to trigger associations that may help you find the correct answer. For example, if a question asks you about the United States' Declaration of Independence, the correct answer is likely to be associated with the revolutionary war period in U.S. history.
- Use the process of elimination to help you find the correct answer. For example, choices referring to, say, Woodrow Wilson or John F. Kennedy are unlikely to be the correct answers to questions about the United States' Declaration of Independence. Your associations with key words in the question can help you to determine and eliminate *wrong* answers as well as find *correct* answers.

As you answer the questions in this book, practice examining the illustrations that accompany them, reading every answer choice, and using key words and the process of elimination. This practice will help you to approach the multiple-choice questions logically and systematically on the day of the actual test.

Consider following these steps.

Step 1 **Read the question carefully and make sure you understand what it is asking.**

By reading carefully, you should be able to determine exactly what the question is asking. It may help you to underline or circle the key words in the question.

Also, watch out for such words as *not* and *except*. These words indicate that you are looking for an exception among the four answer choices.

Step 2 **Examine any chart, graph, map, or other illustration that accompanies the question.**

Examine such illustrations *after* you read the question so that you understand how to use the illustration to answer the question. For example, you may need to find specific information given on the chart, graph, or map, or you many need to come up with a generalization about the information given on the chart, graph, or map. Only the question can tell you how to use the information given!

Step 3 **Read all of the answer choices.**

You may believe that you have identified the correct answer before you have read all of the choices, but read them all to be sure that the answer you have selected is, in fact, the *best* choice. Cross out answer choices as you determine that they are incorrect so that you don't waste time considering them again.

If you cannot determine which choice is correct, use the process of elimination to weed out the bad choices.

You may be able to eliminate three answer choices. Select the remaining choice, because there is a good chance that it is the correct answer.

You may be able to eliminate one or two answer choices. If so, then guess from the remaining choices. By eliminating even one answer choice, you have increased the chances that the choice you select will be the correct answer.

Remember, your associations with key words in the question can help you to determine and eliminate wrong answers.

Step 4 **Record your answer choice and write the answer in the appropriate space on your answer sheet.**

Circle the correct answer choice in your test booklet so that you will remember which choice you decided was correct. Then fill in the appropriate space on your answer sheet. Make sure that you fill in the space for the correct question number and the correct answer choice.

FOR MORE INFORMATION

Check with the Virginia Department of Education for the most recent information about when the SOL assessment in Virginia and U.S. history is given, how it is scored, and what's on it. Visit their Web site for updates:

http://www.pen.k12.va.us/

THE BIG PICTURE

THE BIG PICTURE

The following list contains major people, places, events, and ideas that are likely to appear on the SOL EOC exam in Virginia and U.S. history. The list does not cover everything that's important in U.S. history, nor does it cover everything that will appear on the exam. Rather, the list is a tool that you can use to your advantage. The historical information on the list is the material *most likely* to show up on the test.

Any word, name, or phrase appearing in **bold** within the definitions that follow is listed as its own entry in the Big Picture, which means that its meaning and context are necessary components of any complete definition.

Abolitionists

- Blanket term for those Americans who supported the end of **slavery**
- Most famous leaders were **Frederick Douglass**, **William Lloyd Garrison**, and **John Brown**
- Held some power in Congress, but not enough to outlaw slavery until after the South seceded and the **Civil War** began
- Represented first by the **Liberty Party** and later by the **Free-Soil Party**

Alien and Sedition Acts

- Laws passed during John Adams's presidency
- Restricted naturalization of immigrants and made publishing material critical of the government a crime
- When **Thomas Jefferson** became president, he pardoned everyone imprisoned under the acts and chose not to renew the legislation

American Revolution

- War in which colonists fought the British in an attempt to gain independence
- War officially began with signing of the **Declaration of Independence**
- Fighting began with "the **shot heard 'round the world**"
- Continental Army was led by **George Washington**

Anti-Federalists

- Name for those politicians opposed to ratification of the **Constitution**
- Opposed the creation of a strong federal government
- Supported giving more power to the states and argued that a strong federal government would lead back to tyranny

Armstrong, Neil

- First man to walk on the moon
- Commanded the Apollo 11 mission in August 1969 that met President **John F. Kennedy**'s challenge that **NASA** beat the Soviets to the moon and do so before the end of the 1960s
- Famously said, "That's one small step for a man, one giant leap for mankind," upon stepping onto the moon's surface

Articles of Confederation

- First document to outline a government for the new United States
- Took effect during the **American Revolution**
- Gave power of decisions to the Continental Congress, but reserved most authority for states to decide on their own
- Did not create an **executive branch** of the government
- Created problems because of its weak central government
- Replaced when the **Constitutional Convention** chose not to amend it, but to create the **Constitution** instead

Assembly line

- Manufacturing technique invented by **Henry Ford**
- Uses standardized parts and specialized labor to speed the manufacture of items and thereby lower manufacturing costs
- Allows mass production, which made the **Model T** car affordable and popular in the 1920s

Atomic bomb

- Weapon of mass destruction created by splitting atoms
- Used by the United States against Japan to end **World War II**
- Developed by the secret **Manhattan Project**

Bacon's Rebellion

- 1675 uprising in Virginia
- Led by Nathaniel Bacon, who was unhappy about the colonial government's unwillingness to help settlers on the western frontier protect themselves against American Indians (First Americans)
- Bacon gathered more than four hundred troops and led a rebellion that killed a large number of American Indians
- He turned his sights to the colonial government, deposing the governor and burning down **Jamestown**, which was then the capital of Virginia
- Bacon died in 1676, allowing the previous governor, William Berkeley, to regain control of Virginia

Balance of powers

- Term for the constitutional system wherein different powers are delegated to the three branches of government: **executive** (the president), **legislative** (Congress), and **judicial** (the Supreme Court)

Battle of New Orleans

- Fought in 1814
- Last battle in the **War of 1812**
- Fought two weeks after the British and the Americans had agreed to a treaty
- Massively outnumbered Americans routed an immense British army while sustaining almost no casualties
- Vaulted General **Andrew Jackson** to national fame

Bay of Pigs invasion

- Ill-fated 1961 secret mission to overthrow Fidel Castro's communist government in Cuba
- Authorized by President **John F. Kennedy** just after his inauguration
- Angered the governments of both Cuba and the **Soviet Union** and embarrassed the United States in the eyes of its allies

Bell, Alexander Graham

- Invented the telephone in 1876

Berlin Airlift

- American and British eleven-month joint effort in 1948–49 to supply residents of West Berlin with food and other necessities after the **Soviet Union** blockaded the small, free enclave in the middle of East Germany
- Made Berlin an international symbol of freedom

Berlin Wall

- Constructed by the **Soviet Union** in 1961 to keep East Germans from leaving the country and entering the democratic West Berlin
- Site of President **John F. Kennedy**'s famous visit in 1963
- Destroyed in 1989 when East and West Germany reunified as the Eastern European Bloc of Soviet satellite countries began to fall apart

Bill of Rights

- Collective name for the first ten amendments to the U.S. **Constitution**
- Guarantees that individual rights and liberties are protected from the federal government
- Many states would not ratify the Constitution until a bill of rights was promised
- Written by **James Madison**

Black Power

- Militant movement that grew in the mid- and late 1960s as African Americans lost patience with the slow progress of the nonviolent **Civil Rights movement**
- Advocated by Malcolm X, who was a leader of the black Muslim movement and the Black Panthers, a militant, non-Muslim organization

Black Tuesday

- Day of the stock market crash (October 29, 1929)
- Marked the beginning of the **Great Depression**

"Bleeding Kansas"

- Nickname for the Kansas Territory after Congress decided in 1854 that the status of slaves in Kansas would be decided by **popular sovereignty**
- Earned during the widespread violence that preceded the vote on slavery in Kansas
- The vote was plagued by fraud, as slave owners from neighboring Missouri poured into Kansas to vote
- **John Brown**, a radical **abolitionist**, led a group of men in a massacre of slave owners after the abolitionist town of Lawrence, Kansas, was ransacked

Boston Massacre

- 1770 confrontation between colonists and British troops stationed in Boston
- Colonists taunted and abused soldiers until the soldiers fired into the crowd, killing five colonists
- Colonial rabble-rousers spread propaganda about the incident, portraying the dead as innocent victims and calling the event the Boston Massacre

Boston Tea Party

- In December 1773, a group of colonists under the leadership of the **Sons of Liberty** and disguised as Mohawk Indians boarded a British ship in Boston Harbor and threw its cargo of tea into the harbor in protest
- Protesting the tea tax that was still in place after the repeal of the **Townshend Acts**
- The British responded by passing the **Intolerable Acts** (also known as the Coercive Acts), which, among other penalties, closed Boston Harbor
- As a result, the **First Continental Congress** was convened

Brinkmanship

- American **Cold War** strategy by which conflicts with the **Soviet Union** were allowed to escalate to the verge of war without any negotiation
- Pioneered by President **Dwight D. Eisenhower**'s administration
- Exemplified by the **Cuban missile crisis**

Brown, John

- Radical **abolitionist** leader
- Supported the use of violence to end slavery
- Led a small retaliatory massacre in **"Bleeding Kansas"**
- Led a more famous 1859 raid on the arsenal in Harper's Ferry (then still in Virginia) with the intention of arming slaves for a revolt
- Was arrested, tried, and hanged

Brown v. Board of Education of Topeka, Kansas

- 1954 Supreme Court decision that outlawed **Jim Crow laws** mandating racial segregation in public schools
- First major decision of the **Warren Court**
- Helped inspire the **Civil Rights** movement

Bryan, William Jennings

- Ran unsuccessfully for president three times (1896, 1900, and 1908)
- Most successful campaign was in 1896, as the candidate of the **Democratic** and **Populist** Parties
- Best known as the primary champion of the movement for the **free coinage of silver** (in his "Cross of Gold" speech) and as a leading prosecutor in the **Scopes "monkey" trial** of 1925

Bull Moose Party

- Name taken by the **Progressive** coalition that nominated **Theodore Roosevelt** for president in 1912 after the **Republican Party** nominated William Howard Taft over Roosevelt (who had served twice as a Republican)
- Name came from Roosevelt's self-description: "I am as strong as a bull moose"
- Roosevelt and Taft divided the Republican vote, allowing **Woodrow Wilson**, the **Democratic** nominee, to win

Bush, George H. W.

- Republican president from 1989 to 1992
- Served as vice president under **Ronald Reagan**
- Domestic agenda was largely consumed with trying to fix problems caused by the deficits of the Reagan years
- Foreign policy was crowned by leadership in the **United Nations** coalition that won the **Persian Gulf War**
- Was president when the **Cold War** ended with the fall of the **Berlin Wall** in 1989 and the collapse of the **Soviet Union** in 1991

California gold rush

- Took place when gold was discovered in California in 1849
- Americans who hurried west to find their fortune were thus known as forty-niners
- Increased California's population enough that California became a state decades before any of the Great Plains territories (those between California and the rest of the United States) became states

Carpetbaggers

- Derogatory term for northerners who moved south during **Reconstruction** to make a profit

Civil Rights movement

- Organized campaign for African American civil rights
- Carried out between the mid-1950s and the late 1960s
- Most famous leader was the Reverend Dr. **Martin Luther King Jr.** who advocated nonviolent civil disobedience as the primary tactic to achieve change
- Major events included the Supreme Court's ***Brown v. Board of Education of Topeka, Kansas*** decision, the **Montgomery bus boycott**, the formation of the Southern Christian Leadership Conference (SCLC), the Woolworth's sit-ins, the formation of the Student Nonviolent Coordinating Committee (SNCC), the **March on Washington**, the protest in Birmingham, **Freedom Summer** (1964), the march from Selma to Montgomery, passage of the Civil Rights Act of 1964, the Twenty-fourth Amendment, and the **Voting Rights Act of 1965**

Civil War

- Also known as the War between the States
- Military conflict between the United States (the Union) and the **Confederate States of America** (the Confederacy)
- Fought from 1861 to 1865; the bloodiest war in American history
- **Abraham Lincoln** served as president of the United States during the war
- **Jefferson Davis** served as president of the Confederate States of America
- **Robert E. Lee** led the Confederate Army, while **Ulysses S. Grant** was the last in a series of generals to command Union forces
- The Union eventually won the war, leading to the ratification of the **Civil War Amendments**, the **abolition** of **slavery**, and the onset of **Reconstruction**

Civil War Amendments

- Collective moniker for the Thirteenth, Fourteenth, and Fifteenth Amendments
- Thirteenth Amendment abolished **slavery**
- Fourteenth Amendment granted African American men citizenship and guaranteed all citizens equal protection under the law
- Fifteenth Amendment granted African American men over the age of twenty-one the right to vote
- As a condition of readmission into the Union during **Reconstruction**, the members of the **Confederate States of America** had to ratify these amendments

Cold War

- Term for the extended tensions between the United States and its allies (**NATO**) and the **Soviet Union** and its allies (**Warsaw Pact**)
- Began at the end of **World War II**
- Major events included the **Berlin Airlift**, the **Korean War**, the **Bay of Pigs invasion**, the **Cuban missile crisis**, the building of the **Berlin Wall**, and the **Vietnam War**
- Major American foreign policy ideas relating to the Cold War included **containment**, **brinkmanship**, **deterrence**, the **domino theory**, and **détente**
- Ended during **George H. W. Bush**'s presidency when first the Warsaw Pact and then the Soviet Union dissolved

Columbus, Christopher

- Italian-born explorer who sailed on behalf of Spain
- First European (except for the Vikings) to land in the Americas (the **New World**) in 1492

Common Sense

- Political pamphlet designed to incite colonists to support the move for independence, which would eventually lead to the **American Revolution**
- Published by Thomas Paine in January 1776

Compromise of 1850

- Reached to prevent an imbalance of slave states and free states after a perfect balance had been so carefully maintained, beginning with the **Missouri Compromise** and extending through the next thirty years
- Necessary when President Zachary Taylor suggested disrupting the balance by admitting both California and New Mexico as free states (states where **slavery** would be illegal)
- Maintained peace by creating a package of six laws that admitted California as a free state, divided the Mexican Cession Territory, created the territories of New Mexico and Utah, resolved a boundary dispute between **Texas** and the New Mexico Territory, abolished the slave trade in the District of Columbia, and passed the **Fugitive Slave Act**
- Postponed a sectional crisis between the North and the South for a few more years
- Led to the final split of the **Whig Party**

Confederate States of America

- Formal name of the nation formed by the states in the South after seceding from the United States
- Also known as the Confederacy
- Fought against the northern (Union) states in the **Civil War**
- Original capital was in Richmond, Virginia, although capital was later moved to Montgomery, Alabama, after Union troops took control of Virginia
- Lacked the industrial infrastructure to support a full-scale war against the Union
- Led by President **Jefferson Davis**
- Military was led by General **Robert E. Lee**

Conquistadors

- Name for Spanish explorers who flocked to the **New World** in the sixteenth century
- Sought gold and other treasures and treated the native peoples of Central and South American brutally
- Often accompanied by Catholic missionaries

Conservation

- Notion that the government should withhold certain land from industrial and residential development for the posterity of the nation
- President **Theodore Roosevelt** was widely seen as the champion of conservation, setting aside land for national parks and creating the Forest Service

Constitution

- Document that provides the supreme law for the United States
- Written at the **Constitutional Convention** in 1787, when the **Articles of Confederation** proved ineffective
- Ratified in 1789
- Written by **James Madison**, the "Father of the Constitution"
- Crafted a strong federal government with powers limited by a **system of checks and balances**
- Divides federal government into three branches: **executive**, **legislative**, and **judiciary**
- Has been amended twenty-six times to date (the first ten amendments are called the **Bill of Rights**)

Constitutional Convention

- Meeting convened in Philadelphia in 1787
- Delegates from twelve states met to discuss the problems inherent to the **Articles of Confederation**
- Delegates chose to create a new government by drafting the **Constitution**
- Drafting process was long and arduous, with significant conflicts and compromises, including the early clash between advocates of the New Jersey Plan and advocates of the **Virginia Plan**, as well as the crucial **Great Compromise**
- **James Madison**, who drafted most of the Constitution and is therefore known as the "Father of the Constitution," was a major figure

Containment

- Strategic foundation of the American approach to the **Cold War**
- Held that the United States must work to stop the spread of communism anywhere it might threaten to expand
- Contributed to the **Truman Doctrine**, the **Korean War**, the **Berlin Airlift**, the **Cuban missile crisis**, and the **Vietnam War**, among other policies and events

"Corrupt bargain"

- Nickname for the backroom agreement that allowed John Quincy Adams to win the presidential election of 1824
- When none of the four candidates received a majority of the votes in the **Electoral College**, the final decision fell to the **House of Representatives**
- Henry Clay, who had received the fewest votes of the four candidates, threw his support to the second-place finisher, John Quincy Adams, giving Adams enough votes to defeat the first-place finisher, **Andrew Jackson**
- Adams then appointed Clay to be his secretary of state, a powerful post from which the last four presidents had advanced to the presidency
- Jackson's supporters cried foul, labeling the machinations the "corrupt bargain"
- The outcry weakened Adams and Clay, hindering Adams from accomplishing anything as president and preventing Clay from mounting a credible campaign to become president

Counterculture

- Name for the youth movement in the 1960s that was in opposition to the general principles of the prevailing culture
- Included movements dedicated to liberal politics, feminism, **Civil Rights**, and communal living, in addition to broad agreement on opposition to the **Vietnam War**
- Played major role in the popularity of political rock 'n' roll, including Bob Dylan, the Beatles, and others

Court-packing plan

- President **Franklin D. Roosevelt**'s attempt to put more judges friendly to his **New Deal** agenda on the Supreme Court by adding six additional justices to the Court
- Widely unpopular, the court-packing legislation was defeated in Congress
- Achieved its goal indirectly as the Court reversed its course and ruled in favor of legislation from the Second New Deal

Cuban missile crisis

- 1962 **Cold War** event, triggered when American intelligence discovered Soviet missiles in Cuba and President **John F. Kennedy** appeared on national television to demand the removal of the missiles
- Prime example of **brinkmanship**
- Closest the United States and the **Soviet Union** ever came to war
- Ended when Soviets agreed to remove missiles; in return, the United States agreed not to invade Cuba again (after the **Bay of Pigs invasion**) and secretly agreed to remove American missiles from Turkey

Davis, Jefferson

- President of the **Confederate States of America**

D Day

- Common name for the Allied landing in Normandy, France, during **World War II**
- Allied troops suffered heavy losses but were eventually successful in taking the beach
- From Normandy, the Allies pushed the Germans out of France and most of Belgium, eventually driving the Germans all the way back to Berlin

Declaration of Independence

- Document adopted by the **Second Continental Congress** on July 4, 1776
- Declared the American colonies completely independent of Great Britain, thereby triggering the **American Revolution**
- Drafted by **Thomas Jefferson**
- Jefferson's eloquent expression of many **Enlightenment** social theories made it a groundbreaking document
- Source of famous words, including, "We hold these truths to be self-evident, that all men are created equal, endowed by their creator with certain inalienable rights, and that among these are life, liberty, and the pursuit of happiness"

Democratic Party

- Founded by **Andrew Jackson** when the **Democratic-Republican Party** split after the **"corrupt bargain"** that decided the election of 1824
- Adhered to the basic ideals of **Thomas Jefferson** by favoring **strict construction** of the **Constitution**, a limited federal government, and policies helpful to small farmers
- Was opposed by the **Whig Party**
- The party of Thomas Jefferson, Andrew Jackson, and **Franklin D. Roosevelt**

Democratic-Republican Party

- Political party that developed in opposition to the **Federalists** after the chartering of the **First National Bank**
- Led by **Thomas Jefferson** and **James Madison**
- Advocated a central government empowered to carry out only those functions explicitly enumerated in the **Constitution**
- Fractured after the **"corrupt bargain"** in the election of 1824

Détente

- American **Cold War** policy pioneered by President **Richard Nixon**
- Policy held that working with Cold War enemies to expand trade and create treaties would make war less likely
- Resulted in first American arms treaties with the **Soviet Union** and first official American recognition of the communist government of China

Deterrence

- American **Cold War** policy pioneered by President **Dwight D. Eisenhower**
- Posited that the threat of "massive retaliation"—Eisenhower's term for an American nuclear attack—would prevent the **Soviet Union** from undertaking policies it knew would upset the United States
- Operated as a justification for an increase in the American supply of armaments, particularly nuclear weapons

Dollar diplomacy

- Foreign policy of President William H. Taft (1908–1912) whereby he encouraged American economic **expansion** in Latin American and Caribbean countries by promising and delivering military and economic aid to keep those countries stable and friendly to America

Domino theory

- American **Cold War** concept from President **Dwight D. Eisenhower**'s administration
- Theory that United States must enforce **containment** in third world countries, because once one nation fell to communism, its neighbors would likely follow, just like falling dominoes

Douglas, Stephen

- Senator from Illinois in the years preceding the **Civil War**
- National leader of the **Democratic Party**
- One of the architects of the **Compromise of 1850**
- Creator of the idea of **popular sovereignty** and author of the 1854 Kansas-Nebraska Act that led to "**Bleeding Kansas**"
- Squared off against **Abraham Lincoln** in a famous series of debates (known as the **Lincoln-Douglas debates**) during an 1858 race for a seat in the U.S. **Senate**
- Douglas defeated Lincoln in the Senate race, but lost to him in the presidential election of 1860

Douglass, Frederick

- Former slave who documented his experiences in the famous book *A Narrative of the Life of Frederick Douglass*
- Major organizer and speaker in the **abolitionist** movement

Dred Scott v. Sandford

- 1857 Supreme Court decision on the **Fugitive Slave Act**
- Dred Scott was a slave who had been taken by his master into the Minnesota Territory, which was free territory according to the provisions of the **Missouri Compromise**
- Scott sued for freedom, arguing that residence on free soil made him a free man
- The Supreme Court, led by Chief Justice **Roger Taney,** ruled against Scott
- Decision not only upheld the Fugitive Slave Act, but also held that Dred Scott was not a citizen and had no rights under the **Constitution**, such as the right to seek help from the **judiciary branch** of the government
- Decision caused an uproar in the **abolitionist** movement and added momentum to the sectional strife that led to the **Civil War**

Du Bois, W. E. B.

- African American scholar and political leader most famous for writing the book *The Souls of Black Folk* (1903) and for founding the **NAACP** in 1909

Dust bowl

- Nickname for the terrible conditions that made farming in the Great Plains nearly impossible during the **Great Depression**
- Caused primarily by extended drought and wind, the removal of natural vegetation, and overfarming during **World War I**
- Worst in Oklahoma and northern Texas
- People who left their land and headed to California were known as **Okies**
- Fictionalized in John Steinbeck's *The Grapes of Wrath*

Edison, Thomas

- Inventor known as the "Wizard of Menlo Park"
- He is credited with creating the phonograph, the incandescent lightbulb, and the motion picture camera, among other inventions

Einstein, Albert

- German-born American immigrant
- Famous physicist and teacher
- Convinced President **Franklin D. Roosevelt** to create the **Manhattan Project**
- Famous for his theory of relativity ($E = mc^2$)
- Taught at Princeton University

Eisenhower, Dwight D.

- Republican president from 1953 to 1960
- Was a general in **World War II** and led Allied forces on **D Day**
- Intensified the **Cold War**
- Instituted minimal domestic policy
- Oversaw creation of the interstate highway system
- Warned of the **military-industrial complex**

Electoral College

- Body of electors representing each state; mandated by the **Constitution**
- Electors choose the president based upon the popular vote within their state
- When the Electoral College cannot reach a decision, a final decision is made by the **House of Representatives**
- Until the passage of the Twelfth Amendment in 1804, the Electoral College named the candidate with the second-most electoral votes the vice president
- This system caused trouble in 1796 when **Federalist** John Adams was elected president and **Democratic-Republican Thomas Jefferson** was elected vice president

Emancipation Proclamation

- 1863 edict released by President **Abraham Lincoln**
- Matched the shift in public opinion in the North toward **abolitionism** without actually freeing any slaves, because it officially declared **slavery** outlawed in all land controlled by the **Confederate States of America**, where Lincoln's laws did not hold sway
- Weakened the Confederacy by encouraging African Americans to flee for the North
- Increased morale in the Union, increased foreign support for the Union, and provided a first step to the Thirteenth Amendment, which abolished slavery
- Earned Lincoln the nickname of "the Great Emancipator"

Energy crisis

- Mid-1970s spike in fuel costs that occurred when Middle Eastern oil-producing nations (working together in a group called OPEC) first raised the price of oil considerably and then refused to export oil to nations that supported Israel
- Set off massive inflation in the United States

Enlightenment

- Social movement in Europe during the eighteenth century
- Also known as the Age of Reason
- Characterized by greater emphasis on science, mathematics, logic, and law
- Many of the social theories of the Enlightenment are reflected in the **Declaration of Independence**

Era of Good Feeling

- Nickname for the years during James Monroe's presidency (1817–1825)
- Time when the United States was at peace and had only one political party, the **Federalists** having dissolved
- Not an entirely accurate moniker for a period with its share of problems, including those that led to the issuance of the **Monroe Doctrine**

Executive branch

- One of three branches of the government created by the **Constitution** as part of the **system of checks and balances**
- Headed by the president and the vice president
- Includes all members of the cabinet

Expansionism

- Term applied to the American desire to colonize territory outside of American borders after the close of the frontier in 1890
- Expansionism was carried out in economic, military, political, and social ways
- Prime examples are the **Spanish-American War** and the **Panama Canal**

Fair Deal

- Domestic agenda of President **Harry S. Truman**
- Largely an attempt to continue **New Deal** policies in the years after **World War II**

Federalist Papers, The

- Name for a large collection of essays written pseudonymously by **James Madison**, John Jay, and **Alexander Hamilton**
- Published in a New York newspaper and widely circulated thereafter
- Laid out a strong case for ratification of the **Constitution** and against many of the arguments put forward by the **Anti-Federalists**

Federalists

- Initially, supporters of ratification of the **Constitution** and creation of a stronger central (federal) government than the **Articles of Confederation** allowed
- Under the influence of **Alexander Hamilton**, many Federalists formed a political party during the years of **George Washington**'s presidency
- Centered in New England and led by aristocrats
- Split because of disagreement over federal power and the **First National Bank** and those who left formed the **Democratic-Republican Party**
- Lost power to **Thomas Jefferson** and the Democratic-Republican Party in the election of 1800 (also known as the **Revolution of 1800**), and they never regained power
- Dissolved during the presidency of **James Madison**, in the wake of the **Hartford Convention**

"54° 40' or Fight!"

- Slogan of **James K. Polk** when he ran for president in 1844 on a platform of **manifest destiny**
- Referred to the line of latitude along which Americans wanted the border between the Oregon Territory and Canada drawn
- When Polk annexed **Texas** and got the United States embroiled in the **Mexican-American War**, he was forced to settle with Britain for a less advantageous boundary (at 49°) in the northwest

First Continental Congress

- First widespread organization against British rule in the American colonies
- Was convened in 1774 in Philadelphia in response to the passage of the **Intolerable Acts**
- Twelve colonies (all but Georgia) sent representatives
- Demanded repeal of the Intolerable Acts

First Great Awakening

- Religious revival in the 1740s that spread a more evangelical brand of Protestantism across the colonies, including the popularization of the Baptist and Methodist denominations
- George Whitfield and Jonathan Edwards were the most famous preachers of the time

First Hundred Days

- Special congressional session called by President **Franklin D. Roosevelt** just after his inauguration
- Initiated **New Deal** legislation (for the First New Deal) during this session
- Most productive congressional session in history

First National Bank (First Bank of the United States)

- Chartered by Congress in response to a request from Treasury Secretary **Alexander Hamilton** during **George Washington**'s presidency
- Vociferously opposed as unconstitutional by **James Madison** and **Thomas Jefferson**, who resigned his post as secretary of state because of the bank disagreement
- Disagreement over the bank led to the split between the **Federalists** and the **Democratic-Republican Party**
- Helped the national economy develop by funding the national debts created by the Revolutionary War
- Facilitated the creation of a stable national currency
- Regulated private banks and limited uncontrolled and unprotected economic expansion in the early republic

Flappers
- Stereotype of stylish, emancipated woman of the **Jazz Age**: slim with bobbed hair, short skirts, rolled-down silk stockings, makeup, and sometimes a cigarette
- Actually comprised a very small portion of the population, but still a widely used image in advertisements
- Symbol of the 1920s

Ford, Henry
- Invented the automobile in 1896
- Pioneered the **assembly line**, which revolutionized manufacturing and allowed the **Model T** car to be affordable to most Americans in the 1920s
- Doubled the pay of his workers from $2.50 to $5.00 per day, significantly affecting the economy and leading other industrialists to follow his example

Forrest, Nathan Bedford
- Extremely successful military leader in the **Confederate States of America** army
- After the **Civil War**, he founded the **Ku Klux Klan (KKK)**

Fort Sumter
- American military installation in Charleston Harbor in South Carolina
- **Confederate States of America** troops began the **Civil War** by firing on a Union ship attempting to bring fresh supplies to the soldiers stationed there

Fourteen Points
- Term for President **Woodrow Wilson**'s guidelines for world peace following **World War I**
- Included the end of colonialism and the founding of the **League of Nations**
- Many of Wilson's ideas failed to win international support, and the U.S. **Senate** refused to allow the United States to join the League of Nations, ushering in an era of **isolationism**

Franklin, Benjamin
- One of the Founding Fathers
- Newspaper publisher, civic leader, scientist, inventor, writer, and politician
- Signed the **Declaration of Independence**
- Served as U.S. ambassador to France during **George Washington**'s presidency
- Famous for inventing the lightning rod and for writing *Poor Richard's Almanack* and *The Autobiography of Benjamin Franklin*

Free silver
- Clarion call of the **Populist Party**, a political movement of the 1890s that appealed to rural voters in the West and whites in the South
- Free silver meant the unlimited coinage of American money on the silver standard, as opposed to the gold standard
- Coinage of silver would have reduced farmers' debts by causing inflation
- **William Jennings Bryan** was the great champion of free silver, making it his rallying cry when he ran for president in 1896 election

Free-Soil Party

- Political party that significantly affected American politics in the years before the **Civil War**
- Gathered many **abolitionists** (**William Lloyd Garrison** famously refused to support the party because he thought it was too moderate)
- Drew support from the **Democratic Party** and the defunct **Whig Party**
- Opposed the extension of **slavery** into any territory taken from Mexico and into any territory already declared "free soil" by the **Missouri Compromise**
- Grew out of those who supported the **Wilmot Proviso**
- Replaced the **Liberty Party**
- Fielded candidates in the presidential elections of 1852 and 1856

Freedmen's Bureau

- Federal agency created during **Reconstruction**
- Provided newly freed African Americans with help procuring food, clothing, education, and employment
- Served to help protect African Americans' civil rights
- Was not overwhelmingly effective
- Was extremely unpopular with whites in the South

Freedom Summer

- Major event of the **Civil Rights movement**
- 1964 effort to expand African American voter registration in the South
- Managed to register only 1,200 new voters
- Fifteen Freedom Summer volunteers were killed
- Promoted the need for the **Voting Rights Act of 1965**

French and Indian War

- Also known as the Seven Years' War (1756–1763)
- American colonists and British troops fought the French and American Indian tribes
- American colonists and British won, expanding the western frontier of the colonies
- Followed by the **Proclamation of 1763**

Fugitive Slave Act

- Passed as part of the **Compromise of 1850**
- Guaranteed slave owners the right to capture escaped slaves anywhere in the United States and to claim escaped slaves who were captured by others
- Drew immense criticism from **abolitionists** in the North
- Gave rise to personal liberty laws designed to interfere with the execution of the Fugitive Slave Act in many northern states
- Inspired Harriet Beecher Stowe's famous novel *Uncle Tom's Cabin*
- Upheld by the Supreme Court in the case of ***Dred Scott v. Sandford***

Garrison, William Lloyd

- Most famous **abolitionist** leader
- Published an abolitionist newspaper called *The Liberator*; famed for fiery rhetoric (he called the **Constitution** "an agreement with Hell" because it recognized **slavery**)
- One of the ardent abolitionists who opposed the **Free-Soil Party**

Gettysburg Address

- Famous 1863 speech by President **Abraham Lincoln**
- Delivered at the dedication of a national cemetery for the dead soldiers who fought at the Battle of Gettysburg, one of the bloodiest battles of the **Civil War**
- Contains the famous phrase about the United States having a "government of the people, by the people, for the people"

Gilded Age

- Nickname for the period between the Reconstruction and the turn of the nineteenth century
- Nickname meant to imply that the financial prosperity of the time was only a surface appearance—a gilding—that hid the serious problems within American society

Good Neighbor policy

- American foreign policy toward Latin American and Caribbean nations put forward by President **Franklin D. Roosevelt** during the 1930s
- Reversed interventionist **dollar diplomacy** policies by seeking to develop friendship, trade, and mutual defense
- More about making intervention less obvious than less practiced

Grant, Ulysses S.

- Republican president from 1869 to 1877; oversaw most of **Reconstruction**
- Final general to control all Union forces during the **Civil War**
- Received command in 1864
- After Grant captured Richmond, Virginia, in April 1865, **Robert E. Lee** surrendered at Appomattox Courthouse, Virginia

Great Compromise

- Name for the agreement on state representation in Congress reached at the **Constitutional Convention**
- To strike a balance between large states (who sought representation based upon population) and small states (who sought equal representation for all states), the Great Compromise agreed upon a bicameral legislature, with a "**house of representatives**" dividing representation by population and a **senate** giving equal representation to every state

Great Depression

- Prolonged and powerful economic recession that gripped the United States, beginning with the stock market crash of 1929 (**Black Tuesday**) and extending until **World War II**
- Led to urban unemployment, as well as widespread farm foreclosures because of the **dust bowl**
- Led to the election of President **Franklin D. Roosevelt** and the implementation of **New Deal** legislation that expanded the role of government

Great Society

- Domestic agenda of President **Lyndon B. Johnson**
- Created the broadest array of government-funded social programs since the **New Deal**
- Worked to alleviate economic injustice; often called the War on Poverty
- Included first major successful **Civil Rights** legislation

Hamilton, Alexander

- New York financier who served as treasury secretary during **George Washington**'s presidency
- Designed the economic development of the United States, beginning the **First National Bank**
- Primary leader of the **Federalist** Party
- One of the pseudonymous authors of *The Federalist Papers*
- Was killed in a duel by Vice President Aaron Burr

Harlem Renaissance

- Broad movement of cultural innovation in the African American community during the 1920s
- Introduced important African American novelists, poets, and artists, as well as jazz music, giving the decade the nickname the **Jazz Age**

Hartford Convention

- Gathering of delegates from the New England states in Hartford, Connecticut, in late 1814
- Delegates were unhappy with the progression the **War of 1812**, the decline of the **Federalist Party**, and the diminishing political influence of New England as a region
- Delegates demanded significant revisions to the **Constitution**, but their requests were undercut by the American victory at the **Battle of New Orleans**

Hayes, Rutherford B.

- **Democratic** president from 1877 (after a closely contested election that was deadlocked in the **Electoral College** and was therefore decided in the **House of Representatives**) to 1881
- Won fewer popular votes (and fewer electoral votes) than his opponent—Samuel Tilden—but was elected as part of a political compromise
- Ended **Reconstruction** when he took office in 1877
- First Democrat elected after the **Civil War**

House of Burgesses

- Legislature of colonial Virginia
- First legislative body in colonial America

House of Representatives

- Lower house of the bicameral **legislative branch** established by the **Constitution**
- As a result of the **Great Compromise**, membership in the House of Representatives is proportional to the population of each state
- Currently has 435 members

Immigration

- Arrival of people who are not American citizens and want to settle permanently in the United States
- Reached an all-time high in the mid- and late nineteenth century, because of eastern European immigrants who helped fuel industrial and urban growth in the United States
- Limited by the U.S. government for the first time in the 1920s

Indentured servant

- Person who could not afford passage to the American colonies from Britain and thus promised his or her servitude (usually for a period of seven years) to a "master" who was then willing to pay his or her passage across the Atlantic Ocean
- Became less popular as **slavery** became more widespread

Industrial Revolution

- Term for the period during which the United States converted from an agrarian society (centered on farming and agriculture) to an industrial society (centered on manufacturing and mechanized production)
- Took place in Great Britain in the mid-eighteenth century and in the United States in the nineteenth century
- Initially concentrated in the northeastern U.S. states

Industrialization

- Conversion of the American economy from dependence upon farming to dependence upon manufacturing (i.e., industry)
- Revolutionized the economic, social, and political affairs of the United States, effecting rapid change during the **Gilded Age** and the early decades of the twentieth century

Intolerable Acts

- Colonial nickname for laws known as the Coercive Acts
- Passed by British Parliament in 1774 in response to the **Boston Tea Party**
- Closed Boston Harbor, prohibited colonists from meeting to discuss political or economic matters, and required colonists to provide housing for British soldiers
- Provided the impetus for the **First Continental Congress**

Isolationism

- Term for American withdrawal from European and world affairs in the years following **World War I**
- Ended when the United States entered **World War II**

Jackson, Andrew

- **Democratic** president from 1829 to 1832
- Came to national prominence as a general in the Indian Wars (a series of conflicts with American Indian tribes on the United States' southern and western frontiers) and in the **Battle of New Orleans**
- Nicknamed "Old Hickory"
- Served as a senator from Kentucky
- Lost the presidential election of 1824 because of the **"corrupt bargain"**
- Founded the Democratic Party
- Strengthened the power of the presidency, destroyed the **Second National Bank**, and handled the **Nullification Crisis**
- Instituted the "spoils system," wherein a newly elected president gave federal jobs to supporters of his campaign

Jamestown

- First successful colony in Virginia
- Founded in 1607
- More than two-thirds of the original settlers died during the "starving time" of the first winter
- Site of John Rolfe's first experiment of planting tobacco for export to Great Britain
- Served as the capital of Virginia for many years

Japanese relocation

- Government program during **World War II** under which Japanese Americans who lived on the West Coast were forcibly relocated to internment camps
- Created in response to public concern about espionage
- Resulted in the loss of personal possessions and family businesses by Japanese Americans who were relocated

Jazz Age

- Nickname for the freewheeling 1920s
- Derived from the development of jazz music, which was free and improvisational, as was much of the decade
- Characterized by prosperity, the popularization of entertainment (movies, radio, national magazines, sports, and the automobile), greater reliance upon science, and expanded opportunities for women

Jefferson, Thomas

- One of the Founding Fathers; a Virginian
- Author of the **Declaration of Independence**
- Ambassador to France under the **Articles of Confederation** government
- Author of the 1786 **Virginia Statute on Religious Freedom**
- Secretary of state during **George Washington**'s presidency; resigned in protest of the **First National Bank**
- Founder and leader of the **Democratic-Republican Party**
- Vice president during John Adams's presidency
- Led opposition to the **Alien and Sedition Acts**
- One of the authors of the **Virginia and Kentucky Resolutions**
- Leader of the **Revolution of 1800**
- **Republican** president from 1801 to 1809
- Approved the **Louisiana Purchase** and commissioned the expedition of **Lewis and Clark**
- Founded the University of Virginia and advocated universal public education
- Architect, scientist, inventor, reader, politician, famous thinker
- Donated his book collection to begin the Library of Congress

Jim Crow laws

- System of laws that collectively mandated **segregation** in all areas of life from the 1880s to the 1960s
- Deemed constitutional by the Supreme Court in *Plessy v. Ferguson* (1896), and then deemed unconstitutional in a series of cases decided by the **Warren Court** in the 1950s

Johnson, Andrew

- **Democratic** president from 1865 (when **Abraham Lincoln** was assassinated) to 1869
- Southern slave owner who favored a mild plan for **Reconstruction**
- Had numerous run-ins with Congress, which eventually led to impeachment proceedings against him (he was not charged)
- Despite his objections, Congress instituted **Radical Reconstruction**

Johnson, Lyndon B.

- **Democratic** president from 1963 (when President **John F. Kennedy** was assassinated) to 1968
- Escalated the **Vietnam War**
- Presided over the implementation of **Great Society** legislation
- Pushed **Civil Rights** legislation (Civil Rights Act of 1964 and **Voting Rights Act of 1965**) through Congress
- Served as U.S. senator from Texas before becoming vice president
- Chose not to run for reelection in 1968 because of controversy over the Vietnam War

Joint-stock company

- Company that sold stock to investors to fund exploration and colonization in the sixteenth and seventeenth centuries
- The colony of Virginia was founded by a joint-stock company that earned great dividends for its stockholders from the export of Virginia tobacco to Great Britain

Judicial review

- Practice used by the Supreme Court to determine whether laws passed by Congress are constitutional (i.e., permitted by the **Constitution**)
- First exercised by Chief Justice **John Marshall** in ***Marbury v. Madison***

Judiciary branch

- One of three branches of the government created by the **Constitution** as part of the **system of checks and balances**
- Includes entire federal court system; the highest court is the Supreme Court
- Checks other branches of government through the principle of **judicial review**

Kennedy, John F.

- **Democratic** president from 1961 to 1963, when he was assassinated
- Won an extremely close election over **Richard M. Nixon** in 1960
- Youngest president ever elected and the only Catholic president
- Domestic agenda, called the **New Frontier,** was largely uneventful
- Oversaw the **Bay of Pigs invasion**, the **Cuban missile crisis**, United States' response to the construction of the **Berlin Wall**, and the early escalation of American involvement in the **Vietnam War**
- President **Lyndon B. Johnson** evoked Kennedy's memory to help push **Civil Rights** legislation through Congress

King, Martin Luther, Jr.

- Leader of the **Civil Rights movement**; Baptist minister
- Masterminded the nonviolent civil disobedience strategy of the Civil Rights movement
- Founded the Southern Christian Leadership Conference (SCLC)
- Gave famous "I have a dream" speech at the **March on Washington**
- Assassinated on April 4, 1968, in Memphis
- First individual other than Presidents **George Washington** and **Abraham Lincoln** to have a federal holiday in his honor

King Philip's War

- Led by King Philip, a American Indian tribal leader whose Indian name was Metacom
- Began when King Philip's Wampanoag tribe joined with two other tribes and attacked settlements on the western frontier of New England in 1675 and 1676
- Ended when King Philip was killed in 1676

Know-Nothing Party

- Small political party that advocated a nativist, anti-immigrant, anti-Catholic, and anti-Jewish ideology
- Officially called the American Party, but earned its nickname because, when asked about the party, members answered only, "I know nothing"
- Nominated Millard Fillmore for the presidency in 1856; died out in the 1850s

Korean War

- Conflict early in the **Cold War** in which the United States led a **United Nations** coalition force aiding democratic South Korea in its civil war against communist North Korea
- Ended in a stalemate, as North and South Korea agreed to settle to the borders they had before the Korean War
- Division of Korea into North and South had been caused by Soviet and American occupation during **World War II**

Ku Klux Klan (KKK)

- Secret society organized by whites in the South after the **Civil War** in response to the **Civil War Amendments** and **Radical Reconstruction**; organized by **Nathan Bedford Forrest**
- Used violence to drive out **carpetbaggers** and to intimidate African Americans
- KKK members famously wore white robes and white pointed hoods to disguise themselves
- Later evolved to be anti-Catholic and anti-Jewish, as well as anti–African American
- Still exists today

Labor unions

- Also known as "organized labor"
- Groups composed of working men and women that were first organized in the late nineteenth century to bargain collectively with management for improvements in working conditions, wages, and hours

La Follette, Robert

- Important Progressive politician who served as both a senator from and the governor of Wisconsin
- Pioneered major **Progressive Era** reforms as governor, including the introduction of a graduated income tax and the direct primary election

Laissez-faire

- Philosophy that government regulation of economic activity leads to inefficiency and that competition naturally provides the best regulation for business
- During the **Gilded Age**, American economic policy was theoretically based on laissez-faire policies; although the government refused to regulate business, it aided business by giving industries property and materials

League of Nations

- International organization that was a precursor to the **United Nations**
- President **Woodrow Wilson** suggested the creation of the League of Nations as one of his **Fourteen Points** after **World War I**
- The **Senate** refused to allow the United States to join the League of Nations, signaling the beginning of U.S. **isolationism**

Lee, Robert E.

- Virginian
- Military leader of the **Confederate States of America**

Legislative branch

- One of three branches of the government created by the **Constitution** as part of the **system of checks and balances**
- Bicameral, meaning it is made up of two houses
- Comprised of the **House of Representatives** and the **Senate,** known collectively as Congress
- Responsible for passing laws, declaring war, ratifying treaties, and providing a national budget

Lewis and Clark

- Two explorers (Merriwether Lewis and William Clark) sent by President **Thomas Jefferson** to map and document land acquired in the **Louisiana Purchase**
- Expedition lasted from 1804 to 1806
- Journeyed west from St. Louis all the way to the Pacific Ocean and back
- Received assistance from Indian guide Sacajawea

Liberty Party

- Moderate abolitionist political party
- Fielded candidates in the presidential elections of 1840 and 1844
- Was subsumed by the more successful **Free-Soil Party**

Lincoln, Abraham

- First Republican president, from 1861 to 1865; led country through the **Civil War**
- Began career as a little-known politician from Illinois who challenged **Stephen Douglas** for a seat in the **Senate** in 1858
- **Lincoln-Douglas debates** vaulted him to widespread fame in the North
- Led the Union in the Civil War against the **Confederate States of America**
- Delivered the famous **Gettysburg Address**
- Issued the **Emancipation Proclamation**
- Assassinated by Southern-sympathizer John Wilkes Booth in 1865, before he could implement his modest plan for **Reconstruction**
- Succeeded by **Andrew Johnson**, who was a much less effectual president

Lincoln-Douglas debates

- Series of seven debates between **Abraham Lincoln** and **Stephen Douglas** during the 1858 race for one of Illinois's seats in the **Senate**
- Lincoln forced Douglas to enunciate his position of slavery in the wake of **"Bleeding Kansas"** and *Dred Scott v. Sandford*
- Lincoln's performance in the debates won him widespread fame in the North
- Douglas lost the debates but won the election
- Lincoln's performance set him up for the **Republican Party**'s presidential nomination for the election of 1860 (in which he again ran against Douglas)

Loose construction

- Philosophy of interpreting the **Constitution** broadly and thereby enlarging the scope of the federal government's power beyond the specific enumerated powers
- Opposed by the **Democratic-Republicans**, who preferred a philosophy of **strict construction**

Louisiana Purchase

- 1803 agreement with France to buy all of Louisiana (the French name for all of the land in the Mississippi River Valley) for $15 million
- Doubled the size of the United States
- Negotiated by **James Monroe**
- Approved by President **Thomas Jefferson** in a massive departure from his usual adherence to **strict construction**
- Explored by **Lewis and Clark**

Lusitania

- British luxury liner sunk by German U-boats (submarines) during the early years of **World War I**
- Was smuggling military supplies to the British, but the American press focused its **yellow journalism** on the deaths of 1,200 civilians (128 Americans)
- Its sinking brought the United States to the brink of entering the war, but the United States remained neutral until the **Zimmermann telegram** was intercepted

Madison, James

- Virginian; known as the "Father of the **Constitution**" because he was the primary architect of the **system of checks and balances**; fourth president of the United States (**Democratic-Republican**, 1809–1817)
- Primary advocate of the **Virginia Plan** at the **Constitutional Convention**
- One of the authors of *The Federalist Papers*
- Wrote the **Bill of Rights** as a member of the **House of Representatives**
- Leading congressional critic of the **First National Bank**
- Coauthor of the **Virginia and Kentucky Resolutions**
- Served as secretary of state during **Thomas Jefferson**'s presidency
- Defendant in the seminal Supreme Court case *Marbury v. Madison*
- Negotiated the **Louisiana Purchase**
- President during the **War of 1812**, which was known as "Mr. Madison's War" by its critics
- Advocate of **strict construction** and a leader of the Democratic-Republican Party

Manhattan Project

- Secret program to develop an atomic bomb during **World War II**
- Stationed in New Mexico
- Staffed by a number of famous scientists, including J. Robert Oppenheimer and **Albert Einstein**
- Created the atomic bombs used by the United States against Japan at Hiroshima and Nagasaki

Manifest destiny

- Popular term for mid-nineteenth-century belief that the United States was not only destined, but also obligated to control as much territory in North America as possible (as part of a divine mission to spread democracy, freedom, and Christianity)
- Coined by journalist John O. Sullivan
- Provided the main ideology for the presidential campaign of **James K. Polk**, who supported the annexation of **Texas** and the expansion of the northwest (leading to the rallying cry, **"54° 40' or Fight"**)
- Was a primary motivation for the **Mexican-American War**

Marbury v. Madison

- Lawsuit brought against **James Madison** as secretary of state during **Thomas Jefferson**'s presidency
- William Marbury was a **"midnight appointment"** made by John Adams just before Jefferson's inauguration in the so-called **Revolution of 1800**
- When Madison refused to certify Marbury's appointment, Marbury sued
- Chief Justice **John Marshall**, an ardent **Federalist**, used the case to establish **judicial review**
- Marshall ruled that Marbury deserved his appointment, but also that the Supreme Court lacked the authority to force Madison to certify the appointment
- According to Marshall, the Supreme Court lacked the authority because the Judiciary Act of 1789, which ascribed this power to the Supreme Court, was unconstitutional

March on Washington

- 1963 nonviolent political demonstration; major event of the **Civil Rights movement**
- Brought 250,000 people to the Nation's Capital, making it the largest ever demonstration in the United States at that time
- Site of **Martin Luther King Jr.**'s famous "I have a dream" speech

Marshall, John

- Chief justice of the Supreme Court from 1801 (when he was appointed by President John Adams after the election, but before the inauguration, of **Thomas Jefferson**) to 1835
- Established the principle of **judicial review** (in the famous case of **Marbury v. Madison**), thereby creating an important role for the **judiciary branch** in the **system of checks and balances**
- Succeeded by **Roger Taney**

Marshall Plan

- Massive program of American aid to help European nations rebuild after **World War II**
- Undertaken during the presidency of **Harry S. Truman**
- Helped solidify western European opposition to the **Soviet Union** and the **Warsaw Pact**

Mayflower Compact

- First "constitution" in North America
- Signed by forty-one **Pilgrim** men who came to **Plymouth** on the *Mayflower* in 1620
- Established the rule of law and the **separation of church and state**

McCarthyism

- Nickname for the national witch hunt for communists that took place during the height of the **Cold War**, in the early 1950s
- Named for Wisconsin Senator Joseph McCarthy's leadership in the effort
- Came to an end when McCarthy took on the U.S. Army, which was too powerful for his intimidation tactics
- McCarthy was censured by the Senate in 1954 for his conduct

McCulloch v. Maryland

- 1819 Supreme Court decision in which Chief Justice **John Marshall** asserted the supremacy of federal law over state law
- Decision barred the state of Maryland from levying state taxes on the **Second National Bank**

Mercantilism

- Economic system that promoted the establishment of colonies around the world for the enrichment of European powers during the fifteenth, sixteenth, and seventeenth centuries
- Under this system, colonies exported raw materials to the powerful European "motherland" and then purchased the finished products produced from these raw materials
- Explains why nations were so eager to find, populate, and maintain colonies

Mexican-American War

- Fought from 1846 to 1848
- After annexing **Texas**, the United States claimed a southern border at the Rio Grande, despite the fact that Texans had always claimed a border a couple of hundred miles north, at the Nueces River
- When Mexican troops skirmished with Texans north of the Rio Grande, President **James K. Polk** secured a declaration of war from Congress
- American armies, led by Zachary Taylor (who served as president), routed the Mexicans
- Peace settlement declared the Rio Grande to be the national boundary, ceded California to the United States, and gave the Americans a large tract of land known as the Mexican Cession (later carved into five states), as well as requiring the United States to pay $15 million in unpaid debts to Mexico
- Indicated the popularity of **manifest destiny**
- Led to debates about **slavery** in the Mexican Cession, including debates over the **Wilmot Proviso**

Middle Passage

- Middle leg of the journey from Europe to Africa to America, then back to Europe, by which slaves, along with goods including spices, furs, and gold, were transported
- Name signified the brutal experience of crossing the Atlantic Ocean after being sold or kidnapped into **slavery** from Africa
- Almost 15 percent of slaves did not survive the trip

"Midnight appointments"

- Large number of judicial appointments made by President John Adams the night before **Thomas Jefferson**'s inauguration in the so-called **Revolution of 1800**
- **James Madison** refused to certify a large number of the appointments, leading to the *Marbury v. Madison* court decision, which established the principle of **judicial review**

Missouri Compromise

- Legislative compromise reached in 1820 that preserved the balance of free states and slave states
- Admitted Missouri as a slave state and Maine as a free state
- Banned **slavery** north of the line marked by extending Missouri's southern border all the way west to the Pacific Ocean
- Maintained peace for almost thirty years, until the **Compromise of 1850** was necessary

Model T

- First widely popular automobile in the United States
- Mass-produced by **Henry Ford** in the late 1910s and the 1920s on the **assembly line**
- Its low price led to the popularization of the automobile, which changed the character of American lives and cities in the 1920s (the **Jazz Age**)

Monroe Doctrine

- Foreign policy position announced during James Monroe's presidency
- Declared that the United States would not tolerate European interference in affairs of the Americas, just as the United States would not muddle in European affairs
- Later served as the basis for the **Roosevelt Corollary**

Montgomery bus boycott

- First major demonstration of the **Civil Rights movement**
- Began in 1955 when Rosa Parks, a local employee of the **NAACP**, refused to give her seat on the bus to a white man, in violation of **Jim Crow laws**
- African Americans in Montgomery, Alabama, undertook a boycott of the bus system to protest **segregation**
- Brought local pastor **Martin Luther King Jr.** to national prominence
- Ended a year later when the Supreme Court ruled that segregation on buses was unconstitutional
- Shortly after the boycott, Martin Luther King Jr. founded the Southern Christian Leadership Conference (SCLC), which helped organize the Civil Rights movement

Muckrakers

- Nickname given by President **Theodore Roosevelt** to a group of journalists who worked to expose the abuses of corporate wealth and power in the first years of the twentieth century
- Most famous was Upton Sinclair, whose novel *The Jungle* led to government regulation of the meat-packing industry

National Aeronautics and Space Administration (NASA)

- Government agency that coordinates American exploration of outer space
- Founded by President **Dwight D. Eisenhower**
- Greatest moment was when the Apollo 11 mission landed men on the moon in 1969, meeting President **John F. Kennedy**'s challenge to beat the Soviets to the moon before the end of the 1960s

National Association for the Advancement of Colored People (NAACP)

- Civil rights organization founded by **W. E. B. Du Bois** in 1909
- One of the primary organizations that led the **Civil Rights movement**

Navigation Acts

- Series of acts passed by Parliament between 1651 and 1776 to restrict trade in the American colonies
- Taxed hats, wool, molasses, sugar, and tea, among other duties
- Banned commerce with any nation or colony not part of the British Empire

New Deal

- Domestic agenda of President **Franklin D. Roosevelt** to help lift the United States out of the **Great Depression** in the mid-1930s
- Broken down into the First New Deal (1933–1934) and the Second New Deal (1935–1936), both of which were broad programs regulating business and industry, providing employment through public works programs, and aiding farmers
- Permanently changed the role of the government in American society
- First New Deal was broader in scope but less ambitious in government spending
- After the Supreme Court struck down key parts of the First New Deal, Roosevelt tried to pass his **court-packing plan**
- Second New Deal was more liberal and included significantly more government spending

New Freedom

- Name for Woodrow Wilson's **Progressive** domestic agenda upon which he was elected president in 1912

New Frontier

- Domestic agenda of President **John F. Kennedy**; most of Kennedy's proposals failed to pass through Congress

New World

- Popular name for the Americas in the century after **Christopher Columbus** became the first European to "discover" the area

Nixon, Richard M.

- Republican president from 1969 to 1974
- Served as vice president under President **Dwight D. Eisenhower**, but lost the 1960 presidential election
- Ran unsuccessfully for governor of California in 1962
- Made remarkable political comeback in 1968
- Originated foreign policy of **détente**
- First U.S. president to recognize and visit communist China
- Resigned in disgrace after the **Watergate** scandal enveloped his presidency

North Atlantic Treaty Organization (NATO)

- **Cold War** alliance formed in 1949 by the United States and western European nations for mutual defense against the **Soviet Union** and its communist satellite states, which later signed their own **Warsaw Pact**, creating the Warsaw Treaty Organization

Northwest Ordinance

- Series of ordinances from 1784 to 1787 dividing the American northwest into self-governing territories
- Banned **slavery** in those territories
- Provided that money raised by the sale of land in the territories would be used to fund public education
- Set out requirements for territories to become states

Nullification Crisis

- 1832 crisis that tested the power of the federal government, as designed by the **Constitution**, against states' rights
- Precipitated by congressional renewal of a high tariff on imported goods
- South Carolina passed an ordinance of nullification, declaring the tariff void and threatening secession if the federal government attempted to collect tariff revenue in that state
- In this effort, South Carolina drew heavily on the example of the **Virginia and Kentucky Resolutions**
- President **Andrew Jackson**, who himself supported lowering the tariff, declared nullification "incompatible with the existence of the Union" and sought permission from Congress to use federal troops to enforce the tariff law if necessary
- President Andrew Jackson's response set some precedent for President **Abraham Lincoln**'s reaction to secession at the beginning of the **Civil War**

Okies

- Nickname for farmers who migrated west to California because of the **dust bowl** conditions during the **Great Depression**
- Fictionalized in John Steinbeck's novel *The Grapes of Wrath*

Open Door policy

- U.S. foreign policy toward China at the end of the twentieth century
- Enunciated the American belief that no nation should use its "sphere of influence" in China to limit the trade of any other nation
- No nation agreed to the Open Door policy, but the United States chose to interpret the nonresponses to the Open Door policy as tacit agreement to it

Panama Canal

- Waterway that connects the Atlantic and Pacific Oceans through the Latin American nation of Panama
- Built in the first two decades of the twentieth century after President **Theodore Roosevelt** negotiated American rights to build the canal
- Hallmark achievement of American **expansionism**

Pearl Harbor

- Site of a naval base in Hawaii that was bombed by Japan in a surprise attack on December 7, 1941, leading to U.S. entry into **World War II**

Persian Gulf War

- Fought in 1990 and 1991
- Began when Iraq invaded Kuwait, a small nation that exports a large volume of oil
- President **George H. W. Bush** organized a coalition through the **United Nations** that sent an international force to expel Iraqi troops from Kuwait
- The U.N. force was victorious in only forty-two days

Pilgrims

- Religious dissidents who left England for freedom in the American colonies
- Settled first in Plymouth, Massachusetts
- Traveled on the *Mayflower*, from which their agreement on how to govern the colony, the **Mayflower Compact**, took its name
- Pioneered the concept of the **separation of church and state**
- Separate from the Puritans, who maintained membership in the Church of England, which the Pilgrims had abandoned

Plessy v. Ferguson

- 1869 Supreme Court decision that ruled **segregation** by race was constitutional, as long as "separate but equal" accommodations were available for African Americans
- Laws enforcing segregation were known as **Jim Crow laws**, and they were not widely challenged until the **Civil Rights movement**
- Was overruled by the Supreme Court in the case of ***Brown v. Board of Education of Topeka, Kansas***

Plymouth

- Massachusetts settlement founded by the **Pilgrims** in 1621
- Governed by the **Mayflower Compact**

Polk, James K.

- Democratic president from 1845 to 1849
- Proponent of **manifest destiny**
- Elected on a platform of annexing **Texas** and expanding U.S. land holdings in the northwest ("**54° 40′ or Fight!**")
- Led the United States into the **Mexican-American War**

Popular sovereignty

- Law that allowed the residents of a territory to decide for themselves whether or not they wanted to allow **slavery** in their territory
- Attempt to soothe tensions during the sectional crisis (growing tensions between the North and South) that preceded the **Civil War**
- Part of the **Compromise of 1850**
- Brainchild of **Stephen Douglas**
- Led to the crisis of "**Bleeding Kansas**" when it was the basis for the Kansas-Nebraska Act
- Was a major topic in the **Lincoln-Douglas debates**

Populist Party

- 1890s political party that appealed to western farmers and southern whites by promoting a platform based on the idea of **free silver**
- Reached its height in the 1896 election, when it joined the **Democratic Party** in nominating **William Jennings Bryan** for president

Potsdam

- Site of meeting between Allied leaders Winston Churchill, Joseph Stalin, and **Harry S. Truman** (who had recently become president when **Franklin D. Roosevelt** died) just before the end of **World War II**
- Truman alienated Stalin, contributing to the tension that led to the onset of the **Cold War**

Pre-Columbian era

- Name for the period of history in the **New World** before 1492, when **Christopher Columbus** became the first European to arrive (except for the Vikings' limited explorations)

Proclamation of 1763

- British declaration after the end of the **French and Indian War**
- Prohibited colonists from moving west of the Appalachian Mountains
- Marked the end of **salutary neglect**, which angered American colonists

Progressive Era

- Period beginning in the late nineteenth century and ending with U.S. entry into **World War I**
- Characterized by a movement that prized expanded democracy and greater efficiency as ways to reach economic and social justice
- Supported increased dependence on science and social science
- Worked to alleviate poverty and to expand government regulation of industry

Prohibition

- Banned production, sale, and consumption of alcoholic beverages
- Enacted by the Eighteenth Amendment (1919) and repealed by the Twenty-first Amendment (1933)

Puritans

- Religious dissidents who left England to establish a purer branch of the Church of England
- Settled the Massachusetts Bay Colony in 1630 around the area now known as Boston
- Led by John Winthrop, who envisioned the Puritan society as an example to the world, a "City upon a Hill"
- Separate from the **Pilgrims**, who abandoned the Church of England

Radical Reconstruction

- Term for a series of laws intended to reform the South after the **Civil War**
- Pushed through Congress over the objection of President **Andrew Johnson**
- Established punitive treatment of the former **Confederate States of America**
- Allowed the **Freedmen's Bureau** to use force in meeting its goals
- Required southern states to ratify the **Civil War Amendments** as a condition of readmission to the Union
- Was weakened during the presidency of **Ulysses S. Grant**
- Ended when **Rutherford B. Hayes** became president in 1877

Reagan, Ronald

- Republican president from 1981 to 1988
- Had been a movie actor and then governor of California
- Advocated massive arms buildup in the **Cold War**
- Slashed taxes to fit his theory of supply-side (or trickle-down) economics
- Severely cut government spending in all areas but military expansion
- Instituted deficit spending
- Second term as president was marred by Iran-Contra scandal

Reconstruction

- Term used to describe the years after the **Civil War** but before the resumption of normal operations of the United States (1865–1877)
- Congress set requirements for the readmission of the **Confederate States of America** to the United States
- President **Abraham Lincoln** advocated allowing the southern states back into the Union without too many punitive measures, but he was assassinated before he could implement his plans
- His successor, President **Andrew Johnson**, was ineffectual and seen as far too favorably inclined toward the South
- Over the objections of Andrew Johnson, Congress enforced a series of harsh laws known as **Radical Reconstruction**
- Required each state to ratify the **Civil War Amendments** as a condition of readmission to the Union
- Established the **Freedmen's Bureau**, which was not as effective as planned, leaving many free African Americans to engage in **sharecropping**
- Saw the introduction and rapid spread of the **Ku Klux Klan (KKK)**
- Continued during the presidency of **Ulysses S. Grant**
- Ended after the election of President **Rutherford B. Hayes**

Red Scare

- Recurring fear of communist infiltration in American society
- Occurred first in 1919 and 1920, when U.S. Attorney General A. Mitchell Palmer used Palmer Raids to round up alleged radicals
- Reprised in the 1930s when the House Un-American Activities Committee (HUAC) was formed to investigate communism in the United States
- HUAC shut down the Federal Theater Project of the **New Deal**'s Works Progress Administration
- Resumed again as **McCarthyism** after **World War II**, in the midst of the **Cold War**

Republican Party

- Formed in the mid-1850s by northern **abolitionists** distressed by the passage of the Kansas-Nebraska Act and the incidents in **"Bleeding Kansas"**
- Abolitionists, disappointed that both the **Whig Party** and the **Democratic Party** had agreed to settle for **popular sovereignty**, joined together in the new party
- Nominated John C. Fremont in the election of 1856, and although he lost, he did unexpectedly well in the election
- Nominated **Abraham Lincoln** in the election of 1860
- Dominated American politics from the election of Abraham Lincoln in 1860 through the end of **Reconstruction** in 1877
- One of the two dominant parties in American politics today
- Other famous members included Presidents **Dwight D. Eisenhower**, **Richard M. Nixon**, and **Ronald Reagan**

Revolution of 1800

- Nickname for the transfer of power from the **Federalists** to the **Democratic-Republicans** following the election of **Thomas Jefferson** over President John Adams in 1800
- Also known as the "bloodless revolution" because the government managed to change hands without violence or serious strife
- Biggest controversy in the transfer of power were the **"midnight appointments"** made by John Adams just before he left office

Robber barons

- Nickname given to the wealthiest and most powerful industrialists of the **Gilded Age**

Robinson, Jackie

- First African American to play major league baseball
- Played for the Brooklyn Dodgers beginning in 1947
- Inspired African Americans to work for better treatment and for an end to **segregation**, an early hero of the **Civil Rights movement**
- One of the best baseball players ever

Roosevelt Corollary

- Foreign policy statement issued by President **Theodore Roosevelt** in 1904
- Amplified ideas first enunciated in the **Monroe Doctrine**
- Declared the United States the "policeman" of all affairs in the Western hemisphere
- Response to some economic difficulties in Central and South America

Roosevelt, Eleanor

- Wife of President **Franklin Delano Roosevelt**
- Changed the role of the First Lady by being politically active
- Was "the conscience" of the **New Deal**
- Served as the first U.S. representative to the **United Nations**

Roosevelt, Franklin Delano

- Democratic president from 1933 to 1945 (he died in office, leaving Vice President **Harry S. Truman** to become president)
- Instigated the **New Deal** to help the United States recover from the **Great Depression**
- First president to break the two-term tradition
- Led the United States into **World War II**
- Helped create the **United Nations**
- Organized the **Manhattan Project** to develop the **atomic bomb**
- First president to appoint a woman to his cabinet (Secretary of Labor Frances Perkins)
- Distant cousin of **Theodore Roosevelt**

Roosevelt, Theodore

- Republican president from 1901 (when President William McKinley was assassinated) to 1908
- Gained fame by leading a regiment known as the Rough Riders in the **Spanish-American War**
- First president to enforce the **Sherman Antitrust Act**, earning him the nickname **"trustbuster"**
- Associated with the **Progressive Era**
- Developed domestic agenda known as the **Square Deal**
- Promoted development of the **Panama Canal**
- First president to pursue **conservation** in his policies (he created the Forest Service and set aside land for many national parks)
- Ran for president again in 1912 as the nominee of the **Bull Moose Party**
- Distant cousin of **Franklin D. Roosevelt**

Rosie the Riveter

- Figure portrayed in a popular poster during **World War II**
- Represented women's move into manufacturing jobs during wartime and changing gender roles

Salem witch trials

- Infamous 1692 episode in the **Puritan** town of Salem, Massachusetts, in which more than 170 people were arrested and 20 were executed for allegedly practicing witchcraft
- Most of the testimony came from a group of teenage girls
- Invoked by some as an analogy during **McCarthyism** (playwright Arthur Miller wrote *The Crucible* using this comparison)

Salutary neglect

- Term for the hands-off style of governance that the British maintained over the American colonies during the reigns of Kings George I and George II (1714–1760)
- Contributed to the rise of colonial self-governance
- Ended after the **French and Indian War**, when the British imposed the **Proclamation of 1763** and the **Sugar Act**

Scopes "monkey" trial

- 1925 trial in Tennessee that tried teacher John T. Scopes for violating state law by teaching the theory of evolution
- Received national attention as a conflict between the nation's growing reliance on science and the reassertion of religious fundamentalism
- **William Jennings Bryan** came from Nebraska to prosecute Scopes
- Famous defense attorney Clarence Darrow came from Chicago to defend him on behalf of the newly formed American Civil Liberties Union (ACLU)
- Scopes lost but was fined only one hundred dollars

Second Continental Congress

- Was convened in the spring of 1775, just before **"the shot heard 'round the world"**
- Commissioned and ratified the **Declaration of Independence**
- After the outbreak of the **American Revolution**, appointed **George Washington** general of the Continental Army, oversaw the printing of currency, and drafted the **Articles of Confederation**

Second Great Awakening

- Widespread religious revival that swept the nation between 1790 and 1840
- Provided more opportunities for women to become involved in public life
- Brought about a number of social reform movements

Second National Bank (Second Bank of the United States)

- Institution similar to the **First National Bank** chartered during James Monroe's presidency
- Opposed by agricultural interests in the South and West; strongly opposed by President **Andrew Jackson**
- Jackson vetoed the renewal of the bank's charter, strengthening the presidency by becoming the first president willing to veto a bill for reasons other than questions about its constitutionality
- Jackson then ordered his treasury secretary to withdraw all federal funds from the bank, insistent on shutting the bank down before its charter expired
- When his treasury secretary refused, Jackson appointed another and then another, until he appointed his close friend **Roger Taney**, who did as Jackson wished and was rewarded with an appointment as chief justice of the Supreme Court in 1835

Segregation

- Policy enforced by **Jim Crow laws** that kept African Americans and whites separate in all aspects of public life and many aspects of private life
- Ended by the **Civil Rights movement**

Senate

- Upper house of the bicameral **legislative branch** established by the **Constitution**
- As a result of the **Great Compromise**, membership in the Senate is divided equally among all states
- Currently has one hundred members

Separation of church and state

- Notion that government and religion should function separately
- Established in the **Constitution** by the First Amendment (in the **Bill of Rights**)
- Pioneered by the **Pilgrims** in the **Mayflower Compact** and first entered into American law by **Thomas Jefferson**'s **Virginia Statute on Religious Freedom**

Settlement houses

- **Progressive Era** institutions located in inner-city slums, providing playgrounds, meeting rooms, and educational facilities for local residents, especially women and immigrant families
- Made famous by Jane Addams's account of running a Chicago settlement house, *Twenty Years at Hull House*

Sharecropping

- System that arose during **Reconstruction**
- Freed African Americans who had no land cooperated with landowners who needed labor in the absence of **slavery**
- They agreed that African Americans would farm the land and pay rent by remitting a portion of the harvest to the landowner
- Kept African Americans in crushing poverty, preventing them from leaving the South or moving up in society

Shays's Rebellion

- Grew out of the economic distress that followed the **American Revolution**
- Consisted of a group of debt-ridden farmers in western Massachusetts protesting high taxes
- During the winter of 1786–1787, cold weather and a lack of supplies led to the uprising's disintegration
- Highlighted problems with the **Articles of Confederation** and increased need for the **Constitutional Convention**

Sherman Antitrust Act

- 1890 law designed to regulate business monopolies by outlawing anticompetitive business practices, including trusts and pools
- Enforced poorly until **Theodore Roosevelt** and then William Howard Taft served as presidents; they were known as **"trustbusters"** for their aggressive enforcement of the act
- Was significantly strengthened during President **Woodrow Wilson**'s administration
- Is still in practice today, as evidenced by the recent case against the company Microsoft

"Shot heard 'round the world"

- Unexpected victory of colonial minutemen over the British army in April 1775; marked the unofficial beginning of the **American Revolution**
- Minutemen had been alerted of impending British attack by the famous midnight ride of Paul Revere
- When British marched on Massachusetts towns of Lexington and Concord, heavily outnumbered minutemen inflicted significant losses on the British troops

Slavery

- Practice of buying and selling people from Africa and of African descent as household servants and/or farmworkers
- First practiced in the **New World**, in Virginia, in 1619
- Slaves were imported from Africa, where they were bought or kidnapped, and transported to the Americas by a sea voyage known as the **Middle Passage**
- Slavery in the American colonies was more prevalent in the South than in the North
- Created political problems, beginning with the drafting of the **Constitution** and lasting through the **Civil War**
- Ended by the Thirteenth Amendment (one of the **Civil War Amendments**)

Smith, John

- First governor of the **Jamestown** colony

Social Darwinism

- Sociological theory of the late nineteenth century
- Idea that competition was the natural state of society and that winners in that competition were naturally superior and naturally suited for leadership
- Derived by loosely applying Charles Darwin's theory of evolution to social relations

Social Security

- Government-funded social program created by President **Franklin D. Roosevelt** during the **New Deal** (1935, Second New Deal)
- Provides payments to support the elderly, widows, orphans, and the disabled
- Expanded during the President Lyndon B. Johnson's **Great Society**
- Still an existing and important program in the United States

Sons of Liberty

- Group of colonial activists who organized to incite opposition to British rule in the American colonies
- Founded in response to the **Stamp Act**
- Most famous for their leadership in the **Boston Tea Party**

Soviet Union

- Communist nation that rose to be a world superpower during the **Cold War**
- Had been an American ally in **World War II** but quickly became a rival once the war ended
- Formed protective alliances, including COMECON and the **Warsaw Pact**
- Included Russia and fifteen republics in Eastern Europe and northern Asia

Spanish-American War

- Fought between the United States and Spain in 1898
- Began because of the breakup of Spanish colonial rule in Cuba and accelerated by the effects of **yellow journalism**
- Example of American **expansionism**
- Resulted in American possession of the Philippines, Guam, and Puerto Rico, as well as independence for Cuba
- Also famous for **Theodore Roosevelt** leading the Rough Riders in the Battle of San Juan Hill

Square deal

- Name for President **Theodore Roosevelt**'s domestic agenda, proposed in the 1904 election
- Advocated a "square deal" for both businesses and workers

Stamp Act

- Passed by Parliament in 1764 (shortly after the **Sugar Act**)
- Levied taxes on all documents and printed items
- Intended to raise funds to pay British debts from the **French and Indian War**
- Gave rise to the American cry "No taxation without representation"
- Led to the rise of the **Sons of Liberty**

"Star-Spangled Banner, The"

- Written by Francis Scott Key during the **War of 1812** as a battle took place over Fort McHenry near Baltimore
- Later adopted as the national anthem of the United States

Strict construction

- Philosophy of interpreting the **Constitution** narrowly and thereby limiting the scope of the federal government's authority to those powers specifically enumerated
- Popular with the **Democratic-Republican Party**
- Unpopular with the **Federalist** Party, who preferred **loose construction**

Sugar Act

- Passed by Parliament in 1764
- Increased taxes on sugar and widened the scope of vice-admiralty courts (British courts based in Canada that took precedence over local courts favored by American colonists)
- Along with the **Proclamation of 1763** and the **Stamp Act**, led to increased agitation among American colonists

System of checks and balances

- Underlying theory behind the **Constitution**
- Uses three branches of the federal government—the **executive**, **legislative**, and **judicial** branches—to balance one another and prevent any one branch from gaining too much power
- Designed by **James Madison**

Taft-Hartley Act

- Strongly anti–**labor union** legislation that the Republican-controlled Congress pushed through in 1947
- Repealed large sections of the **Wagner Act**
- Vetoed by President **Harry S. Truman**, who had not been particularly kind to organized labor but said that this bill was too harsh; Congress overrode Truman's veto
- Helped build Truman's campaign to win reelection unexpectedly in 1948

Taney, Roger

- Close friend of President **Andrew Jackson**
- Helped Jackson shut down the **Second National Bank**
- Appointed chief justice of the Supreme Court by Jackson in 1835
- Wrote a number of important decisions, including *Dred Scott v. Sandford*

Texas

- Large area of Mexico that declared its independence in 1836
- Most advocates of Texas independence were Americans who had settled in there
- Leaders of the Republic of Texas advocated annexation by the United States
- The United States waited to annex Texas for the sake of relations with Mexico and because of domestic debates over **slavery**
- **Manifest destiny** became popular, and **James K. Polk** was elected president on a platform of annexing Texas and expanding American territory in the northwest
- Became a state in 1845
- Border dispute with Mexico led to the **Mexican-American War**

Tories

- Nickname for American colonists who were more sympathetic to British rule than to independence and the **American Revolution**

Townshend Acts

- 1768 law of Parliament that imposed new duties on paper, paint, glass, and tea imported into the American colonies
- Used the revenue to pay British government officials working in the American colonies
- Led the colonists to boycott taxed goods and to organize the **Boston Tea Party**

Trail of Tears

- Name for the forced removal of the Cherokee tribe of American Indians from North Carolina to Oklahoma by the U.S. Army in the 1830s
- The Cherokee were forced to walk 1,200 miles west through the winter
- More than 25 percent died along the way

Transcendentalism

- Mid-nineteenth century social, intellectual, and aesthetic movement growing out of the spread of romanticism from Europe to America
- Belief that immersion in nature could allow for a transcendence (a rising above) of daily life
- Important figures include Ralph Waldo Emerson, Nathaniel Hawthorne, Herman Melville, Walt Whitman, Henry David Thoreau, Margaret Fuller, and the painters of the Hudson River School
- Connected to some aspects of the outburst of **utopian experiments**

Transcontinental railroad

- Watershed accomplishment in American history
- Completed in 1869 when two railroads were joined at Promontory Point, Utah, allowing undisrupted railroad travel from the Atlantic Ocean to the Pacific Ocean
- By the end of the nineteenth century, there were a handful of completed transcontinental railroads

Treaty of Paris

- Agreement that ended the **American Revolution**
- Signed in 1783

Triangle Shirtwaist Factory fire

- 1911 fire in a New York City clothing factory
- 146 young female workers were killed because locked doors prevented escape
- Helped convince the public and Congress of the need for reforms in working conditions

Truman Doctrine

- **Cold War** foreign policy that decreed that the United States would provide economic and military aid to any nation attempting to fight against communism
- President **Harry S. Truman** first exercised this principle by asking Congress for $500 million to send to Greece and Turkey in 1947, when Greece was fighting a communist insurrection and Turkey was being threatened by communist expansion

Truman, Harry S.

- Democratic president from 1945 (when President **Franklin D. Roosevelt** died) to 1952
- Made the decision to drop the **atomic bomb** on Japan to end **World War II**
- Led the United States into the **Cold War** after an unsuccessful meeting with Joseph Stalin, the leader of the **Soviet Union**, at **Potsdam**
- Introduced **Cold War** foreign policies of **containment** and the **Truman Doctrine**
- Committed U.S. troops to the **Korean War**
- First president to send U.S. aid to what would become the **Vietnam War**
- Domestic agenda known as the **Fair Deal**
- Won famously close election against Thomas Dewey in 1948
- Promoted civil rights and desegregated the armed forces

Trustbusters

- Nickname given to Presidents **Theodore Roosevelt** and William Howard Taft because of their aggressive enforcement of the **Sherman Antitrust Act**

Turner, Frederick Jackson

- American historian who published famous thesis in 1893, advocating that the American frontier had shaped the American character

Turner, Nat

- African American leader of the largest slave revolt in U.S. history in Virginia in 1831
- Led a band of slaves that swept across the countryside, killing nearly sixty whites before they were captured and executed
- Was convinced that he was a messianic figure

Underground railroad

- Secret network of **abolitionists** and former slaves who helped African Americans escape **slavery** in the South in the years before the **Civil War**
- Most famous leader was former slave Harriet Tubman

United Nations

- International organization founded at the end of **World War II** to help arbitrate international disagreements before they led to wars; agreed upon by Winston Churchill, Joseph Stalin, and President **Franklin D. Roosevelt** at the **Yalta** conference
- Was first convened in San Francisco in 1945
- **Eleanor Roosevelt** served as first U.S. representative to the United Nations

Urbanization

- Trend toward Americans living in cities
- Began accelerating in the **Gilded Age**
- 1920s (the **Jazz Age**) were the first time more Americans lived in cities than in rural areas
- **Immigration** was a major cause

Utopian experiments

- Attempts to create a perfect society
- Swept across the United States in the nineteenth century
- Famous attempts include the Brookfarm (where **Transcendentalists** attempted to live without interference), Oneida, Shaker, and Mormon communities

Vietnam War

- **Cold War** conflict between communist North Vietnam and nationalist South Vietnam, which was supported by the United States
- American advisers aided the South Vietnamese from the presidency of **Harry S. Truman** to the presidency of **John F. Kennedy**, when American military presence in Vietnam expanded
- Was escalated most strongly by President **Lyndon B. Johnson** and then by President **Richard Nixon**, who began secret bombings and invasions of Cambodia
- Extremely controversial in the United States, leading to massive youth protests, the expansion of the **counterculture**, and disarray within the **Democratic Party**, an episode of which was nationally televised at the Democratic convention of 1968
- For the United States, the war ended in 1973, when Nixon agreed to remove American troops, an action that was followed by North Vietnamese takeover of South Vietnam

Virginia and Kentucky Resolutions

- Written by **James Madison** and **Thomas Jefferson**, respectively
- Passed by the state legislatures of these two states
- Resolutions argued that the **Alien and Sedition Acts** were unconstitutional and therefore "unauthoritative, void, and of no force"
- Further argued that the **Constitution** gave the federal government only as much power as was derived from a compact among sovereign states
- Served as basis for states' rights arguments in the **Nullification Crisis** and leading up to the **Civil War**

Virginia Plan

- Introduced at the **Constitutional Convention** by **James Madison**
- Called for a government much like the one outlined by the **Constitution**
- Competed with the New Jersey Plan, which was seen more favorably by small states
- Adapted to accommodate supporters of the New Jersey Plan in the **Great Compromise**

Virginia Statute on Religious Freedom

- 1786 law written by **Thomas Jefferson** and passed by the Virginia legislature
- First law in the United States that required the **separation of church and state**
- Passed after a bill that would have assessed a general tax to support churches—a bill written by Patrick Henry and **George Washington**—was defeated
- Followed by similar laws in New Jersey and New York and, a few years later, by the First Amendment to the **Constitution** (as part of the **Bill of Rights** authored by **James Madison**)

"Virtual representation"

- British response to American colonists' argument against "taxation without representation"
- Meant that each member of Parliament represents the interests of all citizens in the British Empire equally, thereby representing the American colonists despite the colonists' inability to send their own representatives to Parliament
- Argument was roundly mocked by colonial rabble-rousers, including the **Sons of Liberty** and Thomas Paine, author of *Common Sense*

Voting Rights Act of 1965

- Major accomplishment of the **Civil Rights movement**
- Outlawed literacy tests and other voting requirements that kept African Americans from voting, and placed both voter registration and elections under federal jurisdiction
- Pushed through Congress by President **Lyndon B. Johnson**

Wagner Act

- Legislation of the **New Deal** (1935, Second New Deal) signed by President **Franklin D. Roosevelt** that legalized **labor unions**, offered protection to strikers, and regulated working conditions
- Written to replace sections of the National Industrial Recovery Act (NIRA) of the First New Deal
- Large parts of the Wagner Act were repealed by the passage of the **Taft-Hartley Act** during the presidency of **Harry S. Truman**

Wallace, George

- Governor of Alabama during the 1950s and 1960s
- Strong supporter of **Jim Crow laws**
- Ordered state troopers to disrupt the march from Selma in the **Civil Rights movement**
- Garnered almost 10 million votes in a run for president as a segregationist third-party candidate in 1968 against **Richard M. Nixon** and Hubert Humphrey
- Planned to run again in 1972, but was shot and paralyzed the year before

War of 1812

- War fought between the United States and Britain from 1812 to 1814 over trade rights
- Called "Mr. Madison's War" by critics, who blamed President **James Madison** for the war's failures; led critics to meet at the **Hartford Convention**
- Occasion for the composition of "**The Star-Spangled Banner**"
- Ended on a high note for Americans after the **Battle of New Orleans**

War Powers Resolution

- Attempt to restore the **balance of powers** outlined by the **Constitution** after the assumption of presidential (or executive) power during the **Korean War** and the **Vietnam War**
- Passed in 1973
- Requires the president to seek congressional approval within sixty days of the deployment of American troops

Warren Court

- Refers to the Supreme Court during the years that Earl Warren served as chief justice (1953–1969)
- Most famous for its unanimous decision that segregationist **Jim Crow laws** were unconstitutional in *Brown v. Board of Education of Topeka, Kansas*
- Also known as a period of judicial activism and a time of expansion of individual rights
- Other famous cases include the decision guaranteeing that arrested persons be informed of their rights before they are questioned by the police (*Miranda v. Arizona*) and the decision amplifying the right to privacy (*Griswold v. Connecticut*)

Warsaw Pact

- Military agreement between the **Soviet Union** and its communist satellite states to serve as a counterbalance to **NATO**
- Formed in 1955

Washington, George

- First president of the United States (1789–1797); Virginian
- Led the Continental Army during the **American Revolution**; attended the **First Continental Congress**; was elected to commander in chief at the **Second Continental Congress**; presided over the **Constitutional Convention**
- Close friend of **Alexander Hamilton** and a supporter of his economic policies, including the chartering of the **First National Bank**
- Retired rather than seek a third term as president, thus setting the two-term precedent, which was not broken until President **Franklin D. Roosevelt** won a third term in 1940

Watergate

- Scandal that forced **Richard Nixon** to resign from the presidency
- Began when burglars, acting on instructions from the White House, broke into the **Democratic Party** campaign headquarters in the Watergate Hotel before the 1972 election
- The burglars were caught, and the scandal grew out of the White House effort to cover up what had happened
- When Nixon resigned on August 9, 1974, Gerald Ford became president

Whig Party

- Was formed in opposition to the **Democratic Party** when the **Democratic-Republican Party** split after the election of 1824 and the **"corrupt bargain"**
- Initially led by Henry Clay, John Quincy Adams, and Daniel Webster
- Resembled the **Federalist** Party led by **Alexander Hamilton**
- Favored the interests of wealthy urban citizens and businesses over the interests of farmers
- Often nominated famous people with vague political positions as a way to attract votes
- Only successful presidential candidates were war heroes William Henry Harrison and Zachary Taylor

Whiskey Rebellion

- 1792 uprising by western Pennsylvania farmers displeased with the excise tax on whiskey that was one of **Alexander Hamilton**'s economic policies
- Raising cries echoing the French Revolution, the farmers attacked tax collectors
- **George Washington** sent 15,000 federal troops to quash the rebellion, proving that the federal government would not be threatened, but also raising complaints from the **Anti-Federalists**, who were vigilant for signs of tyranny under the new **Constitution**

Wilmot Proviso

- Legislative rider introduced in 1846 by David Wilmot, a member of the **House of Representatives** from Pennsylvania
- Proposed banning the expansion of **slavery** into any land taken from Mexico in the **Mexican-American War**
- Passed in the **House of Representatives** more than a dozen times, but was always defeated in the **Senate**
- Supporters became founders of the **Free-Soil Party**
- Was the issue that finally fractured the **Whig Party**

Wilson, Woodrow

- Democratic president from 1913 to 1920
- Won the three-way 1912 election over William Howard Taft (**Republican Party**) and **Theodore Roosevelt** (**Bull Moose Party**)
- Considered a **Progressive**
- Domestic agenda was known as the **New Freedom**
- Ran for reelection on the slogan "Kept us out of war," but led United States into **World War I** in 1917
- Articulated his famous **Fourteen Points** on postwar world peace and suggested the establishment of the **League of Nations**

Women's suffrage

- Movement to pass federal legislation allowing women to vote; movement had been active since the 1840s
- Led by famous women including Susan B. Anthony and Elizabeth Cady Stanton
- Did not succeed on a national level until the **Progressive Era**, when the Nineteenth Amendment was passed in 1920

World War I

- Fought from 1914 to 1919 between Allied nations (Britain, France, Italy, Russia) and Axis nations (Germany, Austria-Hungary)
- United States joined the war on the side of the Allies in 1917, after the interception of the **Zimmermann telegram**
- Known for its widespread use of technology, including U-boats (submarines), machine guns, gas warfare, tanks, dirigibles (blimps), and airplanes
- Ended with the Treaty of Versailles, which punished Germany and created the **League of Nations**
- U.S. Senate refused to ratify the Treaty of Versailles, beginning the American policy of **isolationism**

World War II

- Fought from 1939 to 1945 between Allied nations (Britain, France, **Soviet Union**) and Axis nations (Germany, Italy, Japan)
- United States joined the war on the side of the Allies in December 1941, after Japan bombed **Pearl Harbor** in Hawaii
- Allies defeated Germany after successful **D Day** invasion
- Allies defeated Japan when United States dropped **atomic bombs** on Hiroshima and Nagasaki
- Led to the **Cold War**

XYZ Affair

- President John Adams sent diplomats to France to negotiate a settlement to trade disagreements between France and the United States
- Public sympathy for France was very high in the United States following the democratic French Revolution
- Adams changed the tide of public opinion by alleging that three French diplomats—whom he identified only as X, Y, and Z—had demanded a bribe from American diplomats before even sitting down to negotiate
- Resulting furor over the XYZ Affair led the United States to the brink of war with France

Yalta

- Site of the last meeting between the leaders of Allied nations in **World War II**—Winston Churchill, Joseph Stalin, and President **Franklin D. Roosevelt**
- Meeting saw great progress, including an agreement on the formation of the **United Nations** and on strategy to end the war against Japan
- Also saw the beginnings of **Cold War** tensions between the United States and the **Soviet Union**
- Followed by meeting at **Potsdam**

Yellow journalism

- Exaggerated and sensationalized journalism common in the late nineteenth and early twentieth centuries
- Designed to persuade and influence public opinion
- Contributed to American involvement in the **Spanish-American War** by sentimentally covering the "suffering" of the Cuban people under Spanish "tyranny"
- Most notably practiced by the Hearst newspapers

Zimmermann telegram

- **World War I** message from Germany to Mexico and Japan that was intercepted by Britain and published in the United States
- Encouraged both Mexico and Japan to declare war on the United States to keep American troops out of World War I
- Led the United States to declare war on Germany and enter World War I

LESSONS AND REVIEWS

LESSON 1
EUROPEAN EXPLORATION AND COLONIZATION

VIRGINIA AND UNITED STATES HISTORY SOL VUS.2 "THE STUDENT WILL DESCRIBE HOW EARLY EUROPEAN EXPLORATION AND COLONIZATION RESULTED IN CULTURAL INTERACTIONS AMONG EUROPEANS, AFRICANS, AND AMERICAN INDIANS (FIRST AMERICANS)."

What This Means

You are expected to understand what happened when Europeans first explored and came to live in the New World. You should know how the Europeans interacted with Africans and American Indians. Think about cultural interactions between these groups, including similarities and differences in customs, food, and art.

Sample

▶ **How did Spanish explorers Hernando Cortes and Francisco Pizarro interact with the cultures they encountered during their explorations of the New World (1519–1525)?**

   A They destroyed and enslaved the Aztec and Incan civilizations.

   B They adopted the customs of the native people in Central and South America.

   C They used the knowledge of the American Indians to ensure the success of the Jamestown colony.

   D They used the techniques of the Aztecs to grow tobacco for profit.

How to Answer

To answer this question, you will have to think about what you know about Cortes and Pizarro and the era in which they explored (the early 1500s). These men were Spanish conquistadors, explorers who journeyed inland from the coasts of Central and South America. The conquistadors were not friendly to the native people they found. Instead, they stole valuables and killed or enslaved many of the native people they met.

During the time that these conquistadors were first landing in the New World, several civilizations were flourishing. Among them were the Aztecs and the Incas.

These empires had complex governments, religions, and cities. Unfortunately, Cortes and Pizarro changed that. The Spanish explorers had no interest in learning from the Aztecs or Incas. Instead, the men destroyed what they found.

Now that you know more about the era in which Hernando Cortes and Francisco Pizarro explored the New World, you can find the answer choice that best captures the conquistadors' behavior.

Answer choice **A** is "They destroyed and enslaved the Aztec and Incan civilizations." You know that Cortes and Pizarro were conquistadors and that these conquistadors destroyed and stole from the native civilizations they encountered in the New World. This answer seems like a good choice, but you should check out the other answer choices before you select this one.

Answer choice **B** is "They adopted the customs of the native people in Central and South America." As conquistadors, Cortes and Pizarro most likely did not respect the Incas and Aztecs or take the time to learn from them. **B** is incorrect.

Answer choice **C** is "They used the knowledge of the American Indians to ensure the success of the Jamestown colony." Europeans did use the knowledge of American Indians to help Jamestown survive. However, this happened about one hundred years later, in North America. **C** is incorrect.

Answer choice **D** is "They used the techniques of the Aztecs to grow tobacco for profit." Cortes never worked with the Aztecs to grow any crop. Conquistadors destroyed native empires instead of cooperating with them. **D** is incorrect. Now that you've considered all of the choices, you should know that **A** is correct.

Even if you don't know the names mentioned in the question, you may know something about the dates that are given. Take a minute to think about the time period the question addresses. Consider the first sample question as an example. Even if you've never heard of Cortes or Pizarro, you may remember that the early 1500s were the very beginning of European exploration of the New World and that this is the era in which the Aztecs and Incas were flourishing. Once you remember what happened to these civilizations, you'll be able to answer the question correctly.

Now You Try It!

Read each question carefully and circle the number that goes with the answer choice you select.

1   The British colonists who established the Jamestown colony in 1607 relied on the food-growing knowledge of—

   A   the recently arrived African slaves

   B   the Spanish conquistadors who had settled in the South

   C   the Powhatan Confederacy of American Indians

   D   the nearby French colonists

2   One way Africans preserved and shared their culture after being forced to come to the New World as slaves in the 1700s was by—

   F   sharing their knowledge of crop rotation

   G   designing and building elaborate artwork

   H   writing their stories down

   J   singing songs from their homelands

3   Interactions between European settlers from Great Britain and American Indians in the 1600s were characterized by—

   A   a rich and friendly exchange of culture and knowledge

   B   brief periods of cooperation followed by violence

   C   long periods of almost no contact at all

   D   mutual respect from both sides

4   Which food products were first grown by American Indians and then shared with European colonists who spread them to other parts of the world?

   F   rice and beans

   G   corn and potatoes

   H   wheat and rice

   J   grapes and olives

5

This map is an early depiction of Virginia. What is the significance of the American Indian names for features of the landscape?

A It shows that Europeans and American Indians shared and overlapped their languages.

B It shows that African culture had a significant impact on European settlers.

C It shows that there was often intermarriage between among Africans, American Indians, and Europeans in the New World.

D It shows that Europeans didn't have to pay American Indians for their land.

6

The picture above shows Powhatan Indian Pocahontas, who married Englishman John Rolfe in 1614. What is the significance of her clothing?

F   It symbolizes the wish of many Europeans to make American Indians convert to their ways and culture.

G   It shows that the American Indians had the same style of clothing and customs as the Europeans.

H   It symbolizes the influence of African culture on the dress of Europeans and American Indians.

J   It shows that Pocahontas was not really an American Indian.

7   **What cultural value did many American Indian tribes demonstrate to Europeans?**

A   personal liberty

B   respect for the environment

C   lack of emphasis of property ownership

D   all of the above

8 What effect did early European colonization have on African cultural traditions during the seventeenth and eighteenth centuries?

F Europeans integrated the African customs into their own way of life, enriching both cultures.

G Europeans encouraged African cultural expression.

H By enslaving and killing many Africans, European colonization made the expression of African culture difficult.

J Europeans carefully preserved African cultural traditions in the New World.

9 European colonization of the Americas resulted in the spread of which religion?

A Christianity

B Judaism

C Islam

D Buddhism

LESSON 2
THE REVOLUTIONARY PERIOD

VIRGINIA AND UNITED STATES HISTORY SOL VUS.4 B,C
"THE STUDENT WILL DEMONSTRATE KNOWLEDGE OF EVENTS AND ISSUES OF THE REVOLUTIONARY PERIOD BY
• DESCRIBING THE POLITICAL DIFFERENCES AMONG THE COLONISTS CONCERNING SEPARATION FROM BRITAIN;
• ANALYZING REASONS FOR COLONIAL VICTORY IN THE REVOLUTIONARY WAR."

What This Means

You must know the main events and issues of the Revolutionary War period. You have to understand the political differences among the colonists regarding the split from Britain. The colonies contained diverse groups of people, and getting them to agree to seek independence was a challenge. You must also understand the reasons the colonists won the Revolutionary War.

Sample

▶ **What role did the French play in the American Revolutionary War?**

A The French supplied Britain with ships and weapons to use against the colonists.

B The French supported the colonists starting in 1778, helping to ensure their victory.

C The French wrote a treaty between the British and the colonists that ended the war.

D The French blockaded Boston, which cut off supplies to the American revolutionaries.

How to Answer

To answer this question, you'll have to identify the major reasons the colonists won the Revolutionary War and recognize what role France had in the conflict. The Revolutionary War began in 1775 with the "shot heard 'round the world" fired at Battles of Lexington and Concord. In 1778, Benjamin Franklin was able to negotiate an agreement whereby France would support the colonists against Britain. This agreement was a major factor in the colonists' eventual victory. The war lasted until 1782, when British government lost the will to fight such an unpopular and expensive war far away from home. The Treaty of Paris settled the terms of the separation from Britain. It was negotiated by Benjamin Franklin, John Adams, and John Jay.

Now that you have had a quick review of the Revolutionary War and France's role in it, look for an answer choice that correctly represents what you've learned.

Answer choice **A** is "The French supplied Britain with ships and weapons to use against the colonists." You know that the French, in fact, did the opposite and helped the colonists. This answer choice is incorrect, and you can eliminate it.

Answer choice **B** is "The French supported the colonists starting in 1778, helping to ensure their victory." The colonists sent Ben Franklin to negotiate an agreement with the French in 1778 to gain their support. This answer seems like a good choice, because you know that French help was one of the three major factors that led to colonial victory. But you should check out the other answer choices before you select this one.

Answer choice **C** is "The French wrote a treaty between the British and the colonists that ended the war." The Treaty of Paris was the agreement negotiated with the British at the end of the war. You know that Ben Franklin, John Adams, and John Jay (who were American colonial leaders) worked with Britain to write the treaty, which granted land and independence to the colonies. But, because the French didn't have a main role in this process, you can eliminate this answer choice.

Answer choice **D** is "The French blockaded Boston, which cut off supplies to the American revolutionaries." Blocking ports with ships is an important war tactic, but you know that the French sided with the American colonial revolutionaries. Instead of cutting them off from supplies, the French gave them supplies. Therefore, this answer choice is incorrect. Now that you've considered all of the answer choices, you should know that **B** is correct.

1.   When you look at answer choices for a multiple-choice question, see if any of them are similar. If you have two answers that are nearly identical, they can't *both* be right, but they *can* both be wrong. Sometimes you can eliminate two incorrect answer choices at once. Consider the first sample question as an example. **A** and **D** are similar in that they both mention the French siding with the British against the colonists. Because France was not the side of the British, it's easy to eliminate both of these answer choices right away.

2.   When you study complex events like an entire war, try to focus on the main reasons for the conflict and its resolution. Focusing on main ideas helps you to understand what was really important and to see trends through history.

Now You Try It!

Read each question carefully and circle the letter that goes with the answer choice you select.

1   **What was the role of African slaves in the American Revolutionary War?**

   A   Thousands of slaves fought in the Continental army in exchange for their freedom after the war.

   B   Slaves in the southern states served the colonial forces as spies in a complex network of communication.

   C   Slaves supported the British by fleeing to England and working on British farms.

   D   Slaves started the war by supporting the Sons of Liberty during the Boston Tea Party.

2   **What was the *main* reason the British eventually surrendered to George Washington and the Continental army in 1781?**

   F   The British had to divert troops to France to fight Napoleon Bonaparte.

   G   The British lost the will to fight an unpopular, costly war on foreign soil.

   H   The British were hugely outnumbered by the colonial army by that time.

   J   The colonists had sunk the majority of England's naval warships.

3   **Why were the Quakers opposed to a war for independence?**

   A   They were loyal to the British government and monarchy.

   B   They were prosperous merchants who depended upon trade with Britain.

   C   They worked for the colonial government, which was funded by Britain.

   D   They were pacifists and opposed violence for any reason.

4   **Which political faction in the colonies opposed seeking independence because they were loyal to the British crown?**

   F   Whigs

   G   Sons of Liberty

   H   Tories

   J   Republicans

5 **Most of the patriots (who favored a revolution for independence) were—**

A white Protestants who owned land and had money

B members of the Anglican Church

C southern plantation owners

D subsistence farmers who were frustrated by taxes

6

What does this drawing tell you about the Battle of Lexington and Concord?

F The American patriots were helped by American Indians.

G The British troops were defeated and forced to retreat.

H The British army was able to overpower the untrained minutemen.

J The American patriots were forced to surrender.

7 Which of the following helped to unite colonists in 1774, particularly in Boston, around the idea of seeking independence?

   A the Navigation Acts

   B Shays's Rebellion

   C the Intolerable Acts

   D the French and Indian War

8

According to the drawing above, what is one reason the British ultimately lost the Revolutionary War?

   F The British soldiers were unorganized in battle.

   G They didn't have weapons as sophisticated as the colonists'.

   H Their straight-line formations made them easy targets.

   J The American Indians were helping the minutemen.

9 What was the *main* reason the patriots wanted to fight for colonial independence?

   A Britain had outlawed slavery, and independence was the only way to keep slaves.

   B They were angry about being repeatedly taxed by Britain without government representation.

   C British rule was threatening the religious freedom of the colonists.

   D They were angry about the Boston Massacre.

10 Why was the Battle of Lexington and Concord called "the shot heard 'round the world"?

   F A group of farmers had repelled an attack from the army of the world's largest empire.

   G The British used the skirmish as an example to the world and killed all the minutemen.

   H It was the battle that won the thirteen colonies their independence.

   J The British battalion fired on the unarmed colonists in unison.

LESSON 3
RATIFICATION OF THE U.S. CONSTITUTION

> **VIRGINIA AND UNITED STATES HISTORY SOL VUS.5 C** "THE STUDENT WILL DEMONSTRATE KNOWLEDGE OF THE ISSUES INVOLVED IN THE CREATION AND RATIFICATION OF THE CONSTITUTION OF THE UNITED STATES AND HOW THE PRINCIPLES OF LIMITED GOVERNMENT, CONSENT OF THE GOVERNED, AND THE SOCIAL CONTRACT ARE EMBODIED IN IT BY DESCRIBING THE CONFLICT OVER RATIFICATION, INCLUDING THE BILL OF RIGHTS AND THE ARGUMENTS OF THE FEDERALISTS AND ANTI-FEDERALISTS."

What This Means

You are expected to understand the issues involved in the creation of the Constitution of the United States. You must understand how the philosophical ideals are reflected in the document. You need to be familiar with the conflicts that took place over its ratification (acceptance by all thirteen states). You must understand the Bill of Rights, as well as the arguments of both the Federalists, who supported a strong central government, and the Anti-Federalists, who were opposed to a strong central government.

Sample

▶ **The Great Compromise during the Constitutional Convention of 1787 was—**

A an agreement that the U.S. Congress would have two bodies, the House of Representatives and the Senate

B a plan by which the Articles of Confederation would be changed through a series of amendments

C an agreement that the three branches of government would have equal power and would be able to check and balance one another

D a plan by which each slave would count as three-fifths of a person when calculating state populations

How to Answer

To answer this question, you must be familiar with the debate surrounding the creation of the U.S. Constitution. When the delegates met in 1787, they knew that they wanted to change the Articles of Confederation, but they disagreed on how to accomplish this goal. First, delegates debated whether to amend the existing articles (the New Jersey Plan) or to create a new and much stronger central government (the Virginia Plan).

Second, the delegates had to decide how each state would be represented in a legislative body. Large states, like Virginia, wanted representation to be based on population. Small states, like Delaware, wanted equal representation.

The Great Compromise was the agreement to make the U.S. Congress *bicameral.* Congress would have two houses, one with the number of representatives based on state population (the House of Representatives) and one with two senators from each state (the Senate).

Because one house of Congress was going to be based on population, southern states wanted slaves to count in their population figures. The northern states objected. This disagreement led to the Three-Fifths Compromise. Each slave would count for three-fifths of a person. These compromises were not perfect, but they enabled the states to come together and form a new, united country.

Now that you have reviewed the main issues of the Constitutional Convention, look for the answer choice that explains the agreement or plan behind the Great Compromise.

Answer choice **A** is "an agreement that the U.S. Congress would have two bodies, the House of Representatives and the Senate." The delegates at the Constitutional Convention did create a bicameral Congress so this answer seems like a good choice, but you should check out the other answer choices before you select this one.

Answer choice **B** is "a plan by which the Articles of Confederation would be changed through a series of amendments." This answer choice is referring to the New Jersey Plan, not the Great Compromise. **B** is incorrect.

Answer choice **C** is "an agreement that the three branches of government would have equal power and would be able to check and balance one another." The Constitutional Convention did design a government with three branches and a system of checks and balances. However, the question asks specifically about the Great Compromise. **A** seems like a better option, so you can eliminate **C**.

Answer choice **D** is "a plan by which each slave would count as three-fifths of a person when calculating state populations." The question of how slaves would be counted was settled by deciding to count each slave as three-fifths of a person, but this agreement was known as the Three-Fifths Compromise. **D** is incorrect. **A** is the right answer.

Tips!

If you read the question and do not immediately recognize a key term, don't give up. For example, consider the sample question. Even if you are not sure exactly what the Great Compromise means, you probably know something about the Constitutional Convention. What problems would the delegates have had to compromise on? How were the states different? Once you take a few moments to consider the issues surrounding a key term, your memory may be jogged so that you can eliminate some of the answer choices and find the correct one.

Now You Try It!

Read each question carefully and circle the number that goes with the answer choice you select.

1   Anti-Federalists including George Mason and Patrick Henry believed that—

   A   slavery should be abolished before the Constitution was ratified

   B   the new Constitutional government had been given too little power

   C   the Constitution created a central government that was too strong

   D   a national bank should be created to stabilize the economy

2   How did the notion of a bill of rights enter into the debate over ratification of the Constitution?

   F   The Constitution's lack of a bill of rights concerned many states and made ratification more difficult.

   G   The strong Bill of Rights had to be changed before delegates at the Convention would vote in favor of the Constitution.

   H   Two factions argued whether the Bill of Rights applied to state governments or just to the federal government.

   J   The Bill of Rights created problems when abolitionists sought to apply it to slaves and thereby challenge the Three-Fifths Compromise.

3 Those delegates who were in favor of ratifying the Constitution convinced citizens of the document's merit by—

A threatening to leave the Union if the United States failed to ratify the Constitution

B publishing *The Federalist Papers,* which explained the need for the new Constitution

C publishing *Common Sense*, a pamphlet which laid out a strong case for a republican form of government

D adding a bill of rights to the new Constitution prior to the ratification debate

4 Federalists including Alexander Hamilton and James Madison believed that—

F the United States should get more involved in foreign affairs, including the French Revolution

G the Constitution should be read literally, meaning the government should take no action not specifically granted by the document

H all government leaders including the president should be elected directly by the people

J a strong central government was favorable and that the new Constitution should be ratified

5 What is one way the principle of limited government was established by the new Constitution?

A The Constitution limited the number of terms any one president could serve in office.

B The Constitution created a two-party system of government.

C The Constitution created three branches of government that could check and balance one another so that no one person or group could become too powerful.

D The Constitution makes it impossible for government leaders to take any action not specifically mentioned in the document.

6 **How is the principle "consent of the governed" embodied in the U.S. Constitution?**

F It established the procedures by which the people would elect their leaders in government.

G It established the procedures by which the government would deal with foreign countries.

H It established a means to admit new states into the union.

J It established a means to amend itself.

7

> We the People of the United States, in Order to form a more perfect Union, establish Justice, insure domestic Tranquility, provide for the common defence, promote the general Welfare, and secure the Blessings of Liberty to ourselves and our Posterity, do ordain and establish this Constitution for the United States of America.

The Constitution begins with the words "We the People." What principle does the preamble illustrate?

A limited powers for the federal government

B separation of church and state

C checks and balances

D government power derived from the consent of the governed

8 How does the concept of *federalism,* as expressed in the Constitution, embody the principle of limited central government?

   F by giving the Supreme Court power

   G by giving the states many powers

   H by establishing the Electoral College

   J by establishing a means of impeachment

9

What does this drawing of the Constitutional Convention show about the conflict between the Federalists and the Anti-Federalists?

   A The conflicts at the Convention were resolved peacefully.

   B The Convention was violent.

   C The Federalist delegates were from the larger colonies.

   D The Anti-Federalist delegates were unruly.

LESSON 4
THE JACKSONIAN ERA

> **VIRGINIA AND UNITED STATES HISTORY SOL VUS.6** "THE STUDENT WILL DEMONSTRATE KNOWLEDGE OF THE MAJOR EVENTS DURING THE FIRST HALF OF THE NINETEENTH CENTURY BY DESCRIBING THE KEY FEATURES OF THE JACKSONIAN ERA, WITH EMPHASIS ON FEDERAL BANKING POLICIES."

What This Means

You are expected to be familiar with the major events and issues of the Jacksonian Era. Andrew Jackson was president of the United States from 1828 to 1836. This standard is focused on federal banking policies, which means you should understand Jackson's opposition to the Second National Bank.

Sample

► **What action sparked the Nullification Crisis during Andrew Jackson's presidency?**

   A Jackson appointed people to whom he owed favors to his cabinet.

   B Jackson vetoed the congressional bill that would have renewed the charter of the Second National Bank.

   C Georgia passed laws forcing the American Indians (First Americans) off their land.

   D The South Carolina legislature passed a resolution stating that federal tariffs were unconstitutional and that the state would not obey them.

How to Answer

To answer this question, you'll have to understand the issues surrounding the Nullification Crisis, a major event of the Jacksonian Era. The Nullification Crisis started when South Carolina challenged the authority of President Jackson and the federal government. The southern states were angry about federal tariffs that benefited the North. They also feared that the federal government was headed in the direction of abolishing slavery. To assert states' rights, Vice President John C. Calhoun wrote a pamphlet. This pamphlet encouraged South Carolina to pass a resolution of nullification, arguing that federal tariffs were unconstitutional and would not be obeyed.

The Nullification Crisis was resolved when Jackson was granted the right to use military force to bring South Carolina into compliance. However, the controversial tariff was also gradually lowered, and the South Carolina legislature repealed the nullification bill.

Now that you have reviewed the details of the Nullification Crisis, look for the answer choice that explains what sparked it. Note that it may be difficult to use the process of elimination with this question because all of the answer choices address actions taken during the Jackson presidency. You must know something about the Nullification Crisis to choose correctly.

Answer choice **A** is "Jackson appointed people to whom he owed favors to his cabinet." Jackson operated his administration according to the spoils system, which means he gave government cabinet positions away to please constituencies who had supported him. This system was part of his effort to strengthen the office of the presidency. It did not spark the Nullification Crisis. You can eliminate this choice.

Answer choice **B** is "Jackson vetoed the congressional bill that would have renewed the charter of the Second National Bank." Andrew Jackson did, in fact, veto this congressional bill. His attack on the Second National Bank was an important event in his presidency, but it was not related to the Nullification Crisis. You can eliminate **B**.

Answer choice **C** is "Georgia passed laws forcing the American Indians (First Americans) off their land." The Jacksonian Era is known for its terrible treatment of American Indians, many of whom were forced off their land. Although Georgia did pass a law, President Jackson did not oppose it. This sad event had nothing to do with the Nullification Crisis and can be eliminated.

Answer choice **D** is "The South Carolina legislature passed a resolution stating that federal tariffs were unconstitutional and that the state would not obey them." South Carolina was asserting the primacy of states' rights when it passed this resolution of nullification. Now that you've considered all of the answer choices, you should know that **D** is correct.

Clues about historical events are often given in their names. For example, the Nullification Crisis has to have something to do with "voiding" or "nullifying" a law. If you are good at vocabulary, take a minute to think about what an event's name says about its importance. Another example is the Trail of Tears. Even if you know nothing about it, you can guess that the term represents some sort of path traveled in sadness.

Now You Try It!

Read each question carefully and circle the number that goes with the answer choice you select.

1 The Second National Bank, chartered during President James Monroe's administration, *primarily* served to—

A collect taxes

B collect funds to pay off American Indians

C stabilize the American dollar

D give loans to new businesses

2 Why did President Andrew Jackson oppose the existence of the Second National Bank?

F It tied up too many federal funds.

G The bank's charter was long expired.

H The Supreme Court had declared it unconstitutional.

J He disliked the rich New Englanders who were behind it.

3 What actions did President Jackson take to dismantle the Second National Bank?

A He vetoed a bill that would renew its charter and withdrew all of its funds.

B He asked Congress to pass a bill that would nullify the Second National Bank.

C He stopped putting funds into the bank and simply waited for it to collapse.

D He sent federal troops to destroy the building.

4 How did President Jackson respond to the Nullification Crisis?

F He appointed his friend Roger Taney to the post of secretary of the treasury.

G He visited the state of South Carolina and persuaded prominent citizens and leaders to repeal the nullification bill.

H He asked Congress to pass a bill that would punish the state of South Carolina with severe fines.

J He asked Congress to pass a bill that would grant him authority to use federal troops to bring South Carolina into compliance.

5

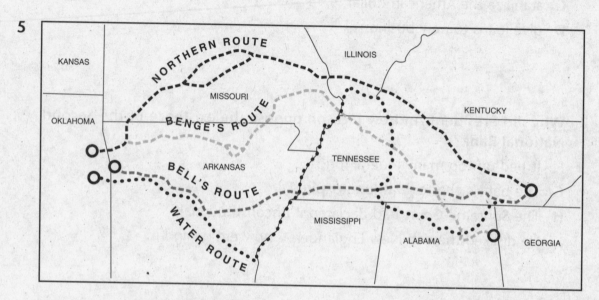

The map above represents—

A the route taken by Louis and Clark

B the Louisiana Purchase

C the Trail of Tears

D the Mason-Dixon Line

6 What was the Trail of Tears?

   F The path on which Andrew Jackson and his troops retreated during the Battle of New Orleans.

   G A forced march of 15,000 Cherokee from their land in Georgia to the Oklahoma Territory, during which 4,000 of them died.

   H The recession caused by the banking fight of Andrew Jackson's first term in office.

   J The front line in the conflict between South Carolina and federal troops after the Nullification Crisis.

7 In regard to relations with American Indians, the Jacksonian Era its characterized as—

   A a violent time in which American Indians were forced off their land or killed

   B a peaceful time in which American Indians and European Americans cooperated

   C a time of war in which American Indians won back most of their land

   D an uneventful time in which American Indians were integrated with white settlers

8 What was Congress's response to President Jackson's actions in regard to the bank fight?

   F They turned to the Supreme Court to decide the constitutionality of a national bank.

   G They officially reprimanded him with a censure resolution that was later repealed.

   H They impeached him.

   J They supported him and passed a resolution officially closing the Second National Bank.

9

What does this political cartoon say about how President Jackson's critics perceived his presidency?

A He acted like a lone ruler without regard for the other branches of government.

B He acted like a weak ruler out of touch with the times.

C He stood up only for the interests of the rich and powerful citizens.

D He was wise and well liked by all.

LESSON 5
THE CIVIL WAR AND RECONSTRUCTION

> **VIRGINIA AND UNITED STATES HISTORY SOL VUS.7 A,B,C** "THE STUDENT
> WILL DEMONSTRATE KNOWLEDGE OF THE CIVIL WAR AND RECONSTRUCTION ERA AND ITS IMPORTANCE
> AS A MAJOR TURNING POINT IN AMERICAN HISTORY BY
> - IDENTIFYING THE MAJOR EVENTS AND THE ROLES OF KEY LEADERS OF THE CIVIL WAR ERA, WITH
>   EMPHASIS ON ABRAHAM LINCOLN, ULYSSES S. GRANT, ROBERT E. LEE, AND FREDERICK DOUGLASS;
> - ANALYZING THE SIGNIFICANCE OF THE EMANCIPATION PROCLAMATION AND THE PRINCIPLES
>   OUTLINED IN LINCOLN'S GETTYSBURG ADDRESS;
> - EXAMINING THE POLITICAL, ECONOMIC, AND SOCIAL IMPACT OF THE WAR AND RECONSTRUCTION,
>   INCLUDING THE ADOPTION OF THE 13TH, 14TH, AND 15TH AMENDMENTS TO THE CONSTITUTION OF
>   THE UNITED STATES."

What This Means

You are expected to understand the Civil War and the time immediately following it,
called the Reconstruction Era. To do this, you should be familiar with major leaders of
the time, as well as major events. You must understand the content and significance
of the Emancipation Proclamation and Lincoln's Gettysburg Address. Finally, you
must understand the effect the war had on political, economic, and social life in the
United States and understand the Thirteenth, Fourteenth, and Fifteenth Amendments
to the Constitution.

Sample

► **What principle was outlined in Lincoln's Gettysburg Address?**

    A the right of all slaves residing in a rebel states to be free

    B the necessity of a government to be responsive to the needs and wishes of
all the factions it serves

    C the value of preserving a union so skillfully created by the Founding Fathers
for the people

    D the importance of building a strong economic platform in the northern states

How to Answer

To answer this question, you have to be familiar with the circumstances of the Battle
of Gettysburg and Abraham Lincoln's basic beliefs regarding the war. The Battle of
Gettysburg in 1863 resulted in massive casualties (approximately 50,000) and turned
the tide of the war firmly in the North's favor. General Robert E. Lee's Confederate
forces had to retreat.

When Lincoln arrived to address a crowd at the battleground in a dedication of a cemetery for the soldiers who had died there, he had a specific duty: He had to explain the importance of continuing with the brutal war. He also had to reiterate the stance of the North, which was preservation of the Union. To make these points, he crafted a short, eloquent speech in which he reminded listeners of the brave actions of the forebears in creating a government that was "of the people, by the people, for the people," promising all who would listen that such a grand experiment would not "perish from the earth."

Now that you have reviewed some details of the Gettysburg Address, look for the answer choice that mentions the principles it contains.

Answer choice **A** is "the right of all slaves residing in a rebel states to be free." Lincoln did grant the slaves freedom during the course of the Civil War, but he did it not in the Gettysburg Address, but in the Emancipation Proclamation. Therefore, **A** can be eliminated.

Answer choice **B** is "the necessity of a government to be responsive to the needs and wishes of the factions it serves." Abraham Lincoln does mention a government of the people, by the people, and for the people in his Gettysburg Address, so this answer might seem like a good choice. However, this is not the main principle he addresses. The Declaration of Independence talks more about this idea, so you can eliminate **B**.

Answer choice **C** is "the value of preserving a union so skillfully created by the Founding Fathers for the people." The Gettysburg Address mentions the country's forebears and the main point of the speech is that the Union must be preserved ("this nation . . . shall not perish from the earth"). This answer seems like a good choice, but you should check out the last answer choice before you select this one.

Answer choice **D** is "the importance of building a strong economic platform in the northern states." The North did have a stronger economy than the South, which was one of the reasons the North won the Civil War. However, Lincoln did not talk about economics during the Gettysburg Address, so this choice can be eliminated. Now that you have considered all the choices, you should know that **C** is correct.

Tips!

1. Since the Gettysburg Address is so famously short, it's a good idea to read it over a couple of times. Like other important documents in American history, it is worth taking the time to learn. Lincoln was an enormously eloquent and intelligent leader. To truly appreciate him, read his words and think about their meaning.

2. The Civil War was a complex event with many major battles and several important leaders. To understand the main ideas, put together a timeline in order to understand the flow of the era. Try to match people with the events so you'll start to automatically pair the prominent generals with their battles.

Now You Try It!

Read each question carefully and circle the number that goes with the answer choice you select.

1 **What was the role of Frederick Douglass during the Civil War era?**

 A A former slave, he fueled the abolitionist movement with his writing and speeches.

 B He was a union general who commanded the army at the battle of Shiloh.

 C An abolitionist leader, he attacked Harper's Ferry to seize the federal arsenal there.

 D He served as the president of the Confederacy for the duration of the Civil War.

2 **Ulysses S. Grant was an important asset to the Union because he—**

 F served as one of Abraham Lincoln's most trusted advisers during the rocky early days of the war

 G was a leading abolitionist who was able to sway public opinion in favor of the war

 H was a skillful general who eventually took command of all Union troops and accepted General Robert E. Lee's surrender at Appomattox

 J was a skillful blockade runner who was able to get supplies and weapons to the North from Europe

3 Which Civil War leader commanded the entire Confederate army from June 1862 until he surrendered in 1865?

A Stonewall Jackson

B Jefferson Davis

C William Tecumseh Sherman

D Robert E. Lee

4 The Emancipation Proclamation was significant because it—

F freed the slaves in rebelling southern states, putting the Union on the side of abolition and inspiring African Americans to join the Union army

G gave slaves the right to vote

H encouraged southern states to secede from the Union, which ultimately began the first hostilities in the Civil War

J served as the blueprint for Reconstruction policies in the South at the conclusion of the Civil War

5 Abraham Lincoln's assassination impacted the South in what way?

A It temporarily stalled the northern war effort, allowing the South to continue fighting for two more years.

B It led the way to Radical Reconstruction, which was harsher than Lincoln's moderate plans for Reconstruction.

C It brought an immediate end to Reconstruction and put southern politicians in control of both the House of Representatives and Senate.

D It ended efforts to enfranchise African Americans in the North and led to the continuation of slavery in the South.

6 Which battle of the Civil War was significant because, as a Union victory, it marked the beginning of the end for the Confederacy?

F Bull Run

G Antietam

H Gettysburg

J Vicksburg

7 The passage of the Fifteenth Amendment during the Reconstruction Era was politically significant because it—

A barred Confederate leaders from holding elected office

B freed the slaves

C blocked states from denying any citizen the equal rights granted by the Constitution

D guaranteed all male citizens over the age twenty-one, including freed slaves, the right to vote

8 Which amendment to the U.S. Constitution officially abolished slavery?

F Thirteenth

G Fourteen

H Fifteenth

J Sixteenth

9

What does this cartoon suggest about the plight of former slaves during Reconstruction?

A They were able to count on the help and protection of the Republicans.

B They were each given forty acres and a mule to get on their feet after the war.

C They continued to be denied basic rights, and Reconstruction did little to help them.

D They were able to become politically active during Reconstruction.

REVIEW 1
LESSONS 1–5

1 What did the passage of the Fourteenth Amendment accomplish?

  A It ended slavery.

  B It ensured that states guaranteed all people born or naturalized in the United States the rights granted by the Constitution.

  C It extended suffrage to women.

  D It granted citizens of the United States the right to a speedy, public, and fair trial by an impartial jury of peers.

2 In what way was Andrew Jackson different from the six presidents who had preceded him?

  F He was a fighter from the west with little schooling who claimed to stand up for the common man.

  G He was the first abolitionist president.

  H He used his presidency to make peace and encourage cooperation with American Indians (First Americans) and new immigrants.

  J He was content to let Congress dictate the policies of the day.

3 During the Civil War, most of the troops from the North were fighting for ____, while most of the southern troops were fighting for ____.

  A the preservation of slavery, the end of slavery

  B states' rights, the end of slavery

  C the preservation of the union, states' rights

  D states' rights, the preservation of slavery

4 Why was getting the states to ratify the new Constitution a difficult task to accomplish?

  F The Constitution significantly curtailed state power by creating a strong federal government.

  G The Constitution set a date for outlawing the institution of slavery.

  H The Constitution gave federal government the power to steeply tax citizens' incomes.

  J The Constitution included a bill of rights that many states considered too radical.

5 Andrew Jackson was easily reelected as president in 1832 because—

A he had a harmonious relationship with most Congressional leaders

B his frontal attack on the Second National Bank was very popular

C southern states knew that he would support their nullification bills

D all of the above

6 What was the *main* reason(s) for colonial victory during the Revolutionary War?

F The British government lost the will to fight a costly and unpopular war on foreign soil.

G The French joined the colonists' side of the war in 1778.

H The Continental army offered freedom to slaves who joined the fight for independence.

J all of the above

7 Which of the following statements about Reconstruction is true?

A It left many freed African Americans trapped in the sharecropping system.

B Its legislation ensured all freed African American southerners a plot of land.

C Its policies helped to curtail the activities of the Ku Klux Klan.

D It lasted from 1865 to 1895.

8 When different groups of people interacted in North America during the seventeenth and eighteenth centuries, which culture dominated and overran the others?

F Asian

G American Indian

H European

J African

LESSON 6
THE EARLY TWENTIETH CENTURY:
EXPANSION, IMMIGRATION, AND DISCRIMINATION

VIRGINIA AND UNITED STATES HISTORY SOL VUS.8 A,C,D

"THE STUDENT WILL DEMONSTRATE KNOWLEDGE OF HOW THE NATION GREW AND CHANGED FROM THE END OF RECONSTRUCTION THROUGH THE EARLY TWENTIETH CENTURY BY

- EXPLAINING THE RELATIONSHIP AMONG TERRITORIAL EXPANSION, WESTWARD MOVEMENT OF THE POPULATION, NEW IMMIGRATION, GROWTH OF CITIES, AND THE ADMISSION OF NEW STATES TO THE UNION;
- ANALYZING PREJUDICE AND DISCRIMINATION DURING THIS TIME PERIOD, WITH EMPHASIS ON "JIM CROW" AND THE RESPONSES OF BOOKER T. WASHINGTON AND W. E. B. DU BOIS;
- IDENTIFYING THE IMPACT OF THE PROGRESSIVE MOVEMENT, INCLUDING CHILD LABOR AND ANTITRUST LAWS, THE RISE OF LABOR UNIONS, AND THE SUCCESS OF THE WOMEN'S SUFFRAGE MOVEMENT."

What This Means

You are expected to be familiar with the issues associated with the end of Reconstruction through the early 1900s. This period was the time in which the United States grew rapidly because of westward expansion, new states, and the growth of cities. You should know about the impact of new immigrants and the Progressive movement, which included the rise of labor unions as well as women's suffrage. The standards also want you to understand the widespread discrimination of the era, especially the Jim Crow laws and the response of African American leaders.

Sample

▶ **What doctrine was established by the U.S. Supreme Court decision of**
   ***Plessy v. Ferguson* in 1896?**

   A Persons placed under arrest must be informed of their legal rights.

   B "Separate but equal" was valid and sufficient to fulfill the rights of African Americans.

   C Neither the states nor the federal government had the right to interfere with the relationship between employer and employee.

   D Slavery could not be banned by the federal government in a territory.

How to Answer

To answer this question, you'll have to identify the principle that was first addressed in the *Plessy v. Ferguson* case. The 1890s were a time of legal racism in which African Americans were treated as second-class citizens. Jim Crow laws limited their rights.

This doctrine was upheld by the Supreme Court in the *Plessy v. Ferguson* case in 1896. The Court ruled that segregation by race was legal. "Separate by equal" facilities were deemed constitutional, but the reality was that accommodations for African Americans were rarely equal. The Jim Crow laws protected by this case existed until the Civil Rights movement began in the 1950s. This decision was overturned by *Brown v. the Board of Education of Topeka, Kansas* in 1954.

Now that you have reviewed the issue associated with the *Plessy v. Ferguson* case, look for the answer choice that explains the doctrine discussed in the previous paragraph.

Answer choice **A** is "Persons placed under arrest must be informed of their legal rights." Because you know that *Plessy v. Ferguson* did not involve the rights of accused criminals, you can eliminate this answer choice. This principle was established by *Miranda v. Arizona.*

Answer choice **B** is "'Separate but equal' was valid and sufficient to fulfill the rights of African Americans." The rights of African Americans were the issue involved in *Plessy v. Ferguson*. Also, you know that the Supreme Court ruled in favor of a "separate but equal" doctrine. This answer seems like a good choice, but you should check out the other answer choices before you select this one.

Answer choice **C** is "Neither the states nor the federal government had the right to interfere with the relationship between employer and employee." The rights of employers and employees were not at issue in *Plessy v. Ferguson*; this principle was established almost ten years later in the *Lochner v. New York* case. Therefore, **C** can be eliminated.

Answer choice **D** is "Slavery could not be banned by the federal government in a territory." By 1896 (the year *Plessy v. Ferguson* was argued), slavery had long been outlawed in all of the United States and its territories. This ban was accomplished by the Thirteenth Amendment to the Constitution. Thus, **D** is clearly incorrect. Now that you've considered all of the answer choices, you should know that **B** is correct.

There are several significant Supreme Court decisions that you might want to take the time to review before the SOL exam. By making yourself familiar with the basic issues associated with landmark cases, you'll be able to answer the questions about them quickly and without hesitation. Don't memorize the exact dates, just think about the doctrines or principles the following cases established:

- *Brown v. Board of Education of Topeka, Kansas* (1954): struck down the "separate but equal" doctrine in public schools
- *Dred Scott v. Sandford* (1857): ruled that slaves were not citizens
- *Marbury v. Madison* (1801): established judicial review of laws
- *McCulloch v. Maryland* (1819): asserted the supremacy of federal law over state law
- *Plessy v. Ferguson* (1896): ruled segregation was legal as long as "separate but equal" accommodations were provided to African Americans

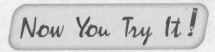

Read each question carefully and circle the number that goes with the answer choice you select.

1   **What action did W. E. B. Du Bois suggest African Americans take to improve their situation in the face of harsh Jim Crow laws?**

   A   send their most gifted students to universities and into the elite white world where they would develop the skills needed to help improve the condition of all African Americans

   B   begin a program of civil disobedience in which unjust laws would be broken and peaceful assemblies would bring attention to the cause of Civil Rights

   C   repeatedly bring cases to court in which instances of separate facilities for African Americans were exposed as being unequal to whites' facilities

   D   improve local communities by attending vocational training

2   **Booker T. Washington was a prominent African American leader during the early twentieth century who encouraged African American citizens to—**

   F   return to Africa

   G   violently protest Jim Crow laws

   H   attend vocational training to improve their communities

   J   move to large cities in the northern United States

3

What does this image suggest about life for African Americans after Reconstruction?

A It was often as brutal and violent as life under slavery.

B It improved a great deal.

C It was a time of great opportunity and change.

D Jim Crow laws protected African Americans from the Ku Klux Klan.

4 In what way did the United States look different in 1900 than it did in 1870?

F Large numbers of people moved south.

G The population moved westward and cities grew.

H Large numbers of people moved out of cities and onto farms.

J The population was less diverse and cities shrank.

5 From the end of Reconstruction through the early twentieth century, territorial expansion and westward movement of the population led to—

A the adaptation of laissez-faire policies

B limits on immigration

C the organization of labor unions

D the admission of new states to the Union

6

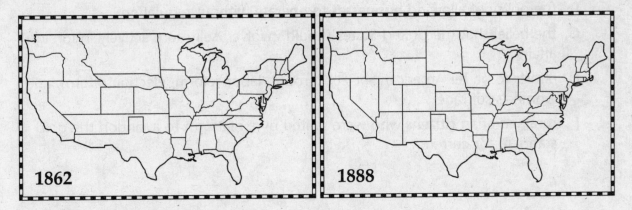

1862

1888

What do the two maps above suggest about the how the United States changed between the Civil War and late 1880s?

F   During this time, large western territories were broken up into the states that exist today.

G   During this time, borders of existing southern states changed.

H   During this time, the area of the country decreased as populations moved east into the largest cities.

J   During this time, several western territories were consolidated into one large territory.

7   **New immigration at the end of Reconstruction through the beginning of the twentieth century helped to fuel—**

A   the growth of cities, the growth of industry, and the rise of labor unions

B   laissez-faire policies, the Civil Rights movement, and the rise of a middle class

C   hostilities between the United States and Europe

D   the American renaissance, the greatest period of literary and artistic production in American history

8 **The Progressive movement was characterized by—**

F the policy of allowing businesses to operate without regulation

G the belief that the United States should involve itself more actively in foreign affairs

H efforts to better American society through labor reform, election reform, and women's suffrage

J rural, agrarian citizens who were united by a platform to abandon the gold standard for currency

9 **Two examples of practices the antitrust laws of the Progressive Era were designed to eliminate are—**

A monopolies and price-fixing by pools

B using child labor and allowing unsafe working conditions

C insider trading and the "spoils system"

D the organization of unions and the bribery of government officials

LESSON 7
WORLD WAR I

VIRGINIA AND UNITED STATES HISTORY SOL VUS.9 B "THE STUDENT WILL DEMONSTRATE KNOWLEDGE OF THE EMERGING ROLE OF THE UNITED STATES IN WORLD AFFAIRS AND KEY DOMESTIC EVENTS AFTER 1890 BY EVALUATING UNITED STATES INVOLVEMENT IN WORLD WAR I, INCLUDING WILSON'S FOURTEEN POINTS, THE TREATY OF VERSAILLES, AND THE NATIONAL DEBATE OVER TREATY RATIFICATION AND THE LEAGUE OF NATIONS."

What This Means

You are expected to know how the role of the United States in world affairs changed when the country became involved in World War I. To understand this period in history, you must be familiar with President Woodrow Wilson's Fourteen Points. You should understand the controversies surrounding the Treaty of Versailles, the agreement that ended the First World War. You must also understand the reasons the United States failed to support the League of Nations.

Sample

▶ **As World War I neared its end, President Woodrow Wilson presented his Fourteen Points, which—**

    A explained his reasons for entering the war on the side of the Allies

    B would harshly punish Germany by demanding steep payments to Allied nations

    C outlined goals, such as ending colonialism, for reaching a peace settlement

    D were ultimately used verbatim in the Treaty of Versailles

How to Answer

To answer this question, you'll have to understand how World War I came to an end and a peace agreement was reached. When the United States entered the war in 1917, the tide turned in favor of the Allies. Germany realized that victory was impossible as its partners in the war—Bulgaria, Turkey, and Austria-Hungary—all surrendered. To save its land from invasion, Germany arranged an armistice. It was signed on November 11, 1918. As these events occurred, President Woodrow Wilson articulated his Fourteen Points, which outlined goals for an official peace settlement. His two main goals were the end of colonialism and the establishment of the League of Nations. Wilson's Fourteen Points did not end up being the ultimate model for a peace agreement, however, as the European Allies chose instead to go in a different direction and use the opportunity to severely punish Germany.

Now that you have reviewed some details about the end of World War I, look for the answer choice that best explains Wilson's Fourteen Points.

Answer choice **A** is "explained his reasons for entering the war on the side of the Allies." President Woodrow Wilson appeared before Congress in 1917 to ask for a declaration of war against Germany, and Congress did declare war on Germany on April 6, 1917. He did not present his Fourteen Points at the beginning of U.S. involvement, however, so this answer choice can be eliminated. Wilson simply stated that the aim of U.S. involvement was to "make the world safe for democracy."

Answer choice **B** is "would harshly punish Germany by demanding steep payments to Allied nations." European Allies Britain and France did want to punish Germany severely at the end of World War I, but this action was not part of Wilson's plan for reaching peace. Therefore, this answer choice can be eliminated.

Answer choice **C** is "outlined goals, such as ending colonialism, for reaching a peace settlement." Wilson's Fourteen Points did outline goals for reaching a peace settlement at the conclusion of World War I. One of the goals was, in fact, ending colonialism. This seems like a good choice, but you should check out the last answer choices before you select this one.

Answer choice **D** is "were ultimately used verbatim in the Treaty of Versailles." You know that Wilson's Fourteen Points were not used word for word in the Treaty of Versailles peace agreement because Britain and France wanted to move in the direction of punishment. **C** is clearly a better option, so **D** can be eliminated. Now that you've considered all of the answer choices, you should know that **C** is correct.

When you answer questions during the SOL exam, it may be tempting to rush. However, take a moment to read all of the answer choices. Consider the sample question. All of the answer choices are closely related to World War I, so you have to read them all to make sure you choose correctly. If you had simply matched Wilson's Fourteen Points with the answer choice containing another key phrase from that era, the Treaty of Versailles, you would have gotten the question wrong.

Read each question carefully and circle the number that goes with the answer choice you select.

1   Prior to World War I, American foreign policy under Presidents William McKinley, Theodore Roosevelt, and William Howard Taft could be characterized as—

A   eurocentric

B   isolationist

C   expansionist

D   benevolent

2   Why did the United States get involved in World War I after several years of neutrality?

F   The United States was swayed to enter the war when it found out about the Holocaust.

G   The United States had always been unofficially on the side of the Central Powers and entered the war because of fears that they were about to lose.

H   The United States wanted to acquire colonial territory controlled by Germany.

J   The United States suffered losses from German submarine attacks and was selling goods and lending money to the Allies.

3   What were the *main* points of the Treaty of Versailles (1919)?

A   It disarmed Germany and took away some of its territory, demanded steep repayments to the Allies, and established the League of Nations.

B   An economic alliance of European nations was formed with the end goal being the establishment of a common currency.

C   It set up new borders in Europe, forming the nations of Czechoslovakia and Yugoslavia from what had been the Austria-Hungary empire.

D   It ended colonialism in Asia and Africa by granting independence to several principalities and set up the League of Nations.

4 The U.S. Senate did *not* ratify the Treaty of Versailles because—

F it felt that the punishment of Germany called for in the treaty was too severe

G it objected to the treaty's provisions for ending colonialism

H it was concerned that the League of Nations would override American interests

J it felt the League of Nations would be ineffective because it didn't have the power to punish a nation that broke the rules of the organization

5

Stop him!

This propaganda poster appeared in the United States during World War I. Which of the following *best* describes its purpose?

A to encourage Americans to enter the war to defeat the German menace

B to convince Americans to ration goods during the war

C to encourage Americans to buy war bonds to fund the war

D to reassure Americans that the world was safe

6 During the national debate over whether to ratify the Treaty of Versailles and join the League of Nations, President Woodrow Wilson—

   F spoke out against the Treaty of Versailles and its ratification because it differed too much from his Fourteen Points

   G traveled across the country urging citizens to write to their congressmen in favor of the treaty and the League of Nations

   H spoke out against the Treaty of Versailles because the League of Nations it established was too weak

   J did not participate in the discussion because he was involved in running for reelection

7 What was the goal of the League of Nations?

   A to keep peace in the world

   B to unite European nations economically

   C to end Communism

   D to aid underdeveloped nations

8 How did involvement in World War I change the U.S. economy?

   F The war started a period of globalization in which tariffs were lowered and new products flooded the domestic market from abroad.

   G The war sparked an economic boom and positioned the United States as a world power.

   H The war enhanced progressive policies of the previous decade, empowering the middle class.

   J The war sparked a recession that lasted through most of the 1920s.

Europe in 1914
Before World War I

Europe in 1921
After World War I

What was one major change in the political map of Europe as a result of World War I?

A The Austria-Hungary empire was broken up into smaller countries.

B France gained significant territory.

C Italy's northern border was moved south.

D The new Soviet Union occupied most of Europe.

LESSON 8
WORLD WAR II

VIRGINIA AND UNITED STATES HISTORY SOL VUS.10 A,B,C,D,E

"THE STUDENT WILL DEMONSTRATE KNOWLEDGE OF WORLD WAR II BY

- IDENTIFYING THE CAUSES AND EVENTS THAT LED TO AMERICAN INVOLVEMENT IN THE WAR, INCLUDING MILITARY ASSISTANCE TO BRITAIN AND THE JAPANESE ATTACK ON PEARL HARBOR;
- DESCRIBING THE MAJOR BATTLES AND TURNING POINTS OF THE WAR IN NORTH AFRICA, EUROPE, AND THE PACIFIC, INCLUDING MIDWAY, STALINGRAD, THE NORMANDY LANDING (D DAY), AND TRUMAN'S DECISION TO USE THE ATOMIC BOMB TO FORCE THE SURRENDER OF JAPAN;
- DESCRIBING THE ROLE OF ALL-MINORITY MILITARY UNITS, INCLUDING THE TUSKEGEE AIRMEN AND NISEI REGIMENTS;
- DESCRIBING THE GENEVA CONVENTIONS AND THE TREATMENT OF PRISONERS OF WAR DURING WORLD WAR II;
- ANALYZING THE HOLOCAUST (HITLER'S "FINAL SOLUTION"), ITS IMPACT ON JEWS AND OTHER GROUPS, AND POSTWAR TRIALS OF WAR CRIMINALS."

What This Means

This standard requires you to understand the relationship the United States had with Great Britain before World War II and understand the reasons the United States finally entered the war. Although you will probably not be asked about the details of specific battles, you need to know where major battles, like Midway and Stalingrad, occurred and how they affected the outcome of the war. Minorities played an important part in the American war effort and you need to understand the contributions of the African American "Tuskegee Airmen" and the Japanese American Nisei regiments, who fought for the United States even though many Japanese Americans were being placed in internment camps. You will need to know the importance of the Geneva Conventions and understand how they relate to the treatment of prisoners during the Second World War. Finally, you must understand what the Holocaust was and be able to explain both its impact on Jewish people worldwide and the Nuremburg trials that followed the war.

Sample

▶ **The purpose of the Normandy landing on D Day was—**

A to push the Germans out of France

B to join Russian troops battling German forces on the Eastern European front

C to take Italy and convert it to the side of the Allies

D to get back at Japan for the Pearl Harbor attack three years earlier

---

How to Answer

To answer this question, you'll need to understand what the Normandy landing on D Day accomplished. Prior to this event, the only active fighting on land in Europe was taking place in the east, in the Soviet Union. The Soviets wanted Allies from the United States, Britain, and Canada to open a second front in the European war. By landing in Normandy (on the west coast of France), the Allies established this second front, drawing Germans into a battle in the west and ultimately forcing them out of Paris and France altogether by September. Meanwhile, Soviet troops pushed Germany back from the east, and the Nazi menace was contained. The D Day invasion is remembered as one of the most significant events in World War II, because it marked the beginning of the end for the Third Reich.

Now that you have reviewed some details about D Day, look for the answer choice that explains the purpose of the invasion.

Answer choice **A** is "to push the Germans out of France." The Normandy invasion on D Day did result in the end of German occupation of France. This answer seems like a good choice, but you should check out the other answer choices before you select this one.

Answer choice **B** is "to join Russian troops battling German forces on the Eastern European front." The Normandy invasion occurred on the west coast of France, so it was quite far from the Eastern European front. Because the Normandy invasion opened a second front instead of joining the existing battles, you can eliminate this answer.

Answer choice **C** is "to take Italy and convert it to the side of the Allies." Mussolini's government fell from power in 1943 after the Allies' North African victories. This answer choice is incorrect.

Answer choice **D** is "to get back at Japan for the Pearl Harbor attack three years earlier." Because the Normandy invasion occurred in France and was aimed at containing the German threat, this answer choice is clearly wrong. Now that you've considered all of the answer choices, you should know that **A** is correct.

To better understand the major battles and turning points in World War II, you might want to locate the place names on a world map. By associating Normandy with the European theater in the west, you can immediately eliminate two of the four answer choices. Do the same with Midway, Stalingrad (St. Petersburg), and Pearl Harbor.

Now You Try It!

Read each question carefully and circle the number that goes with the answer choice you select.

1 **Prior to direct involvement in World War II, the United States made it clear which side it was on by—**

A sending warships to aid France and Belgium

B providing military assistance to Britain on the lend-lease program

C developing the atomic bomb for Great Britain

D lending money to China and providing military goods to Japan

2 **What was the direct result of the Japanese attack on Pearl Harbor on December 7, 1941?**

F The United States entered World War II.

G The alliance between Japan, Germany, and Italy was dissolved.

H The Soviet Union entered World War II.

J The tide of World War II turned in the favor of the Allies.

3 **The Battle of Midway in 1942 was significant because it—**

F resulted in the fall of Paris to German occupation

G resulted in the end of Mussolini's reign in Italy

H marked a turning point in the European theater

J marked a turning point in the Pacific theater

4 **What military goal did President Harry S. Truman accomplish with the decision to drop the atomic bomb in 1945?**

A He forced the surrender of Germany without a ground invasion.

B He forced the surrender of Japan without a ground invasion.

C He turned the tide of the war in Europe in the Allies' favor.

D He convinced the Soviet Union to end its military action in Asia.

5 Which of the following U.S. military units was composed of all African American men and flew missions primarily in the European theater during World War II?

A Resistance Air Force

B Green Berets

C Tuskegee Airmen

D Lincoln Brigade

6

> (1.) Persons taking no active part in the hostilities . . . shall in all circumstances be treated humanely . . .
>
> To this end the following acts are and shall remain prohibited at any time and in any place . . . :
>
> (a) violence to life and person, in particular murder of all kinds, mutilation, cruel treatment and torture;
>
> (b) taking of hostages;
>
> (c) outrages upon personal dignity, in particular, humiliating and degrading treatment;
>
> (d) the passing of sentences and the carrying out of executions without previous judgment pronounced by a regularly constituted court affording all the judicial guarantees which are recognized as indispensable by civilized peoples.
>
> (2.) The wounded and sick shall be collected and cared for.
>
> An impartial humanitarian body, such as the International Committee of the Red Cross, may offer its services to the Parties to the conflict.

The provisions above regarding treatment of prisoners of war were agreed upon at—

F the Geneva Conventions

G the United Nations

H the Yalta Conference

J Normandy

7 Hitler's "final solution" that ended the lives of eleven million Jews, gypsies, homosexuals, political dissidents, people with handicaps, and many other groups is called—

A chemical warfare

B the atomic bomb

C the Holocaust

D the Geneva Conventions

8

Concentration Camp Extermination Camp

North Sea · Denmark · Sweden · Baltic Sea · Lithuania · Latvia · Russia · Belarus · Neth. · Poland · Germany · Czech Republic · France · Slovakia · Ukraine · Switzerland · Austria · Hungary · Romania · Moldova · Italy · Slovenia

What does this map suggest about Hitler's efforts to exterminate the Jews in Europe during the World War II Holocaust?

F The Holocaust took place in three locations.

G Hitler's efforts were limited to camps in Poland.

H Hitler's efforts were limited to camps in Germany.

J The Holocaust took place in camps all over Europe.

9 **The Nisei regiments were the most decorated in American military history, with more than five thousand medals and no deserters, despite heavy casualties. This segregated unit was made up of—**

A Japanese Americans

B American Indians

C African Americans

D women

LESSON 9
THE AFTERMATH OF WORLD WAR II

VIRGINIA AND UNITED STATES HISTORY SOL VUS.11 A,B,C,D "THE STUDENT WILL DEMONSTRATE KNOWLEDGE OF THE EFFECTS OF WORLD WAR II ON THE HOME FRONT BY
- EXPLAINING HOW THE UNITED STATES MOBILIZED ITS ECONOMIC, HUMAN, AND MILITARY RESOURCES;
- DESCRIBING THE CONTRIBUTIONS OF WOMEN AND MINORITIES TO THE WAR EFFORT;
- EXPLAINING THE INTERNMENT OF JAPANESE AMERICANS DURING THE WAR;
- DESCRIBING THE ROLE OF MEDIA AND COMMUNICATIONS IN THE WAR EFFORT."

What This Means

The Second World War had a huge impact on the lives of the Americans who, for whatever reason, did not go overseas and fight. You are expected to understand the impact of World War II on the "home front" in the United States. One major change was the mobilization of the United States' economic might to focus on the war. In order to keep wartime production at a high level, American businesses had to replace many of their white, male workers (who were off fighting the war) with women and minority workers. This employment led to new economic opportunities for many Americans. You must also understand the role of the media in supporting, reporting, and justifying the war. Finally, you should be familiar with the internment of Japanese Americans during the war.

Sample

▶ **During World War II, which group of Americans on the West Coast was forced to sell all of their possessions, close their businesses, and relocate to assigned camps?**

A American Indians (First Americans)

B German Americans

C African Americans

D Japanese Americans

How to Answer

To answer this question, you need to be familiar with the reasons behind the shameful internment of Japanese Americans during World War II.

After the United States declared war on Japan, West Coast citizens started worrying about spies. Many feared that Japanese Americans would place loyalty to their homeland over loyalty to their adopted home. Anti–Japanese American suspicions were not founded upon any hard evidence; rather, these suspicions were a result of years of distrust between Asian immigrants and Americans who had moved west.

The Supreme Court ruled twice that it was legal to force more than 100,000 Japanese Americans into internment camps, where conditions were very poor. These Americans had only days to sell their homes, businesses, and possessions before relocation. No Japanese American was ever charged with espionage. In 1988, Congress paid each surviving internee $20,000 in restitution.

Now that you have reviewed the details of the internment of Japanese Americans during World War II, you should be able to answer the sample question.

Answer choice **A** is "American Indians (First Americans)." American Indians have suffered much persecution throughout American history, including being pushed off their land onto undesirable reservations. American Indians, however, were never interned during World War II. You can eliminate this choice.

Answer choice **B** is "German Americans." The United States was at war with Germany during World War II, but German American citizens were not interned in large numbers during the war. This choice can be eliminated.

Answer choice **C** is "African Americans." African Americans were not interned during World War. This choice can be eliminated.

Answer choice **D** is "Japanese Americans." You know that citizens on the West Coast, where many Japanese Americans lived, were worried about spies and were distrustful of Asian immigrants. Now that you have considered all of the choices, you should know that **D** is correct.

Tips!

1. Some SOL questions are concerned with social issues, which means they address how groups of people were affected by historical events. Social history deals with how people lived their day-to-day lives and how society changed during times of flux. This section is mainly concerned with social history: how World War II affected the lives of minorities and how the home front mobilized to support the war effort. To better understand recent social history, take the time to talk to your parents, grandparents, and other adults about their memories of a certain time period.

2. Sometimes questions contain clues to the answer. For example, the sample question includes the phrase "on the West Coast." This is significant because you know that many Asian immigrants stayed in this part of the United States, including Japanese Americans. Take the time to read every word in a question carefully.

Now You Try It!

Read each question carefully and circle the number that goes with the answer choice you select.

1   **In response to the outbreak of World War II, women contributed to the war effort in all of the following ways** *except*—

    A joining the armed forces in combatant roles

    B taking jobs in heavy industry to meet the needs of wartime production

    C rationing goods including food, shoes, nylons, and gasoline

    D piloting planes that ferried supplies as part of WASP (Women Airforce Service Pilots)

2   **What social effect did the participation of African Americans in the labor force and armed forces have during World War II?**

    F Historical prejudice and Jim Crow laws in the South largely disappeared as Americans united against foreign enemies.

    G Civil rights organizations like NAACP and CORE greatly expanded, as the seeds of the Civil Rights movement were sown.

    H African Americans moved out of cities en masse.

    J African Americans took on a greater role in government by running for office and electing large numbers of African American representatives to Congress.

3 Which minority group was allowed to serve in all phases of the armed forces?

A women

B Japanese Americans

C African Americans

D Mexican Americans

4 To ensure that the military had all the materials it needed to fight World War II, Americans on the home front had to—

F volunteer their time working in factories

G donate their cars and appliances to the government

H ration goods like meat, sugar, rubber, nylon, and gasoline

J move from single family homes to large apartments

5 How did media such as popular Hollywood films help the war effort during World War II?

A The media boosted morale among troops and on the home front with patriotic content.

B The media convinced citizens in neutral nations to join the Allies.

C The media brought the latest news, uncensored, from the frontlines to the home front.

D The revenues the media generated were given to the war effort for new supplies.

6 In order to mobilize the funds necessary for World War II, the U.S. government—

F received loans from foreign nations

G articulated the Marshall Plan

H passed the Servicemen's Readjustment Act, known as the G.I. Bill

J sold war bonds and expanded the income tax

7 To ensure the United States had the military resources necessary to fight World War II, American factories—

A were taken over and run by the federal government

B expanded production to meet wartime needs

C relied on child labor

D shut down production for the duration of the war

8 Which of the following activities was *not* part of the home front effort to win World War II?

F blackout drills

G drives to sell war bonds

H rationing of gasoline and other fuels

J the organization of minutemen militias

9

Do with less—
so they'll have
enough!

RATIONING GIVES YOU YOUR FAIR SHARE

This World War II poster encourages American citizens to—

A buy American products

B ration products

C buy war bonds

D enlist in the armed forces

10 What type of media did President Franklin D. Roosevelt use to conduct his "fireside chats" with the nation?

F television

G newspaper

H radio

J film

REVIEW 2
LESSONS 6–9

1

> Suffrage for women
>
> Child labor laws
>
> Election reform
>
> Prohibition

The above list includes some of the main goals and accomplishments of—

A the Populist movement

B the Progressive movement

C the New Deal

D the Social Darwinist movement

2 **How did Jim Crow laws affect the lives of African Americans in the late nineteenth and early twentieth century?**

F The laws ensured that African Americans did not have to pay federal taxes.

G The laws prevented African Americans from leaving the southern states.

H The laws ensured that African Americans received forty acres and a mule during Reconstruction.

J The laws segregated African Americans from whites and treated them as second-class citizens.

3 **Who were the "muckrakers"?**

A people who helped maintain a government policy of laissez-faire toward industry

B journalists who worked to expose abuses of corporate power

C women in favor of suffrage

D industrialists who opposed labor unions

4 **Why was the battle of Stalingrad significant during World War II?**

F It was the largest battle of the war, resulting in the greatest loss of life of any ground conflict in history.

G It was the turning point in the Allies' favor in the Pacific theater of World War II.

H It was the first time German troops successfully captured and occupied foreign land during the war.

J It was the turning point of the war in the Allies' favor in the Eastern European front.

5 Which of the following battles marked the Allied invasion of western Europe during World War II?

A Normandy

B Pearl Harbor

C Stalingrad

D Hiroshima

6

What does this popular poster tell you about the role of women in World War II?

F Women stayed home or served as nurses in World War II.

G Women did not play a large role in the war effort.

H Women were instrumental in the war by working in heavy industry.

J Women served in all parts of the military during World War II.

7 The United States emerged from World War II as the most powerful nation in the world because—

A it had relatively few casualties

B it did not endure sustained ground fighting on its soil

C its major cities were never bombed

D all of the above

LESSON 10
U.S. FOREIGN POLICY
SINCE WORLD WAR II

VIRGINIA AND UNITED STATES HISTORY SOL VUS.12 A,B,C,D "THE
STUDENT WILL DEMONSTRATE KNOWLEDGE OF UNITED STATES FOREIGN POLICY SINCE WORLD WAR II BY

- DESCRIBING OUTCOMES OF WORLD WAR II, INCLUDING POLITICAL BOUNDARY CHANGES, THE
  FORMATION OF THE UNITED NATIONS, AND THE MARSHALL PLAN;
- EXPLAINING THE ORIGINS OF THE COLD WAR, AND DESCRIBING THE TRUMAN DOCTRINE AND THE
  POLICY OF CONTAINMENT OF COMMUNISM, THE AMERICAN ROLE IN WARS IN KOREA AND VIETNAM,
  AND THE ROLE OF THE NORTH ATLANTIC TREATY ORGANIZATION (NATO) IN EUROPE;
- EXPLAINING THE ROLE OF AMERICA'S MILITARY AND VETERANS IN DEFENDING FREEDOM DURING THE
  COLD WAR;
- EXPLAINING THE COLLAPSE OF COMMUNISM AND THE END OF THE COLD WAR, INCLUDING THE ROLE
  OF RONALD REAGAN."

What This Means

After World War II, the United States, spared the destruction and devastation inflicted
on the major nations in western Europe, was one of the two "superpowers" of the
world. The other superpower was a wartime ally turned rival, the Soviet Union. From
the 1950s to the late 1980s, the United States and communist countries such as
the Soviet Union and Maoist China engaged in a "cold war" around the globe. The
United States and its allies would spread democratic and free market ideals while at
the same time attempting to check the spread of communism. The United States'
efforts to stop the spread of communism became the key component of the U.S.
foreign policy of "containment."

To understand this period in history, you must be familiar with how World War II
ended, meaning that you should understand how boundaries of countries changed
and how the Marshall Plan helped Europe. You are expected to understand U.S.
foreign policy—how the government interacts with other nations—since World War
II. You need to be able to make the connection between the American policy of
containment and American involvement in NATO. You should be able to explain
American involvement in the Korean War and the Vietnam War. Finally, you should
be familiar with the key reasons for the collapse of the Soviet Union during the
Reagan administration.

Sample

▶ **What principle regarding U.S. foreign policy did the Truman Doctrine set forth during the post–World War II era?**

  A The United States would not involve itself in European affairs as long as Europe stayed out of the Western hemisphere.

  B The United States would aid all free nations struggling against communism.

  C The United States planned to act as a police officer in North and South America.

  D The United States would give massive monetary aid to democratic European nations rebuilding after World War II.

How to Answer

To answer this question, you'll have to identify the policy that was articulated by the Truman Doctrine. The post–World War II era was a time of dominance for the United States, but this economic and political supremacy was threatened very early by the rise of the communist Soviet Union. As a rival superpower, the Soviet Union attempted to expand its own sphere of influence and power in Eastern Europe and Asia. When President Truman asked Congress in 1947 for money to support those people in Greece who were fighting communists, he said that it must be the policy of the United States to aid all free peoples struggling against communism.

This declaration resulted in a policy of "containment" that lasted for several decades. Containment meant that the United States would show resistance at every point in the world where the Soviet Union was attempting to expand.

Now that you have reviewed the details of the Truman Doctrine, look for an answer choice that explains the foreign policy principle discussed in the previous paragraph.

Answer choice **A** is "The United States would not involve itself in European affairs as long as Europe stayed out of the Western hemisphere." This sentence more clearly illustrates the Monroe Doctrine, a nineteenth-century foreign policy. The Monroe Doctrine, named for President James Monroe, represented an effort to keep Europe out of North and South American affairs. During World War II, the United States was, obviously, heavily involved in European affairs and unlikely to give up its influence there after fighting stopped. Therefore, **A** can be eliminated.

Answer choice **B** is "The United States would aid all free nations struggling against communism." Because the Truman Doctrine was set forth in 1947, when the United States was just starting to view the Soviet Union as its chief rival, this answer seems like a good choice. However, you should check out the other answer choices before you settle on this one.

Answer choice **C** is "The United States planned to act as a police officer in North and South America." In the post–World War II era, U.S. foreign policy reached far beyond the Western hemisphere, concerning itself more with Europe and the spread of communism in Asia.

Answer choice **D** is "The United States would give massive monetary aid to democratic European nations rebuilding after World War II." This answer seems like a good choice because you know that the United States did give monetary aid to Europe after World War II. However, this policy was known as the Marshall Plan and can be eliminated because it doesn't explain the principle of the Truman Doctrine. Now that you've considered all the choices, you should know that **B** is correct.

This section covers a large time period in U.S. history (1945–1988), but focuses on only one aspect of that era—foreign policy. When you look at an SOL question, think about whether it is concerned with cultural history, social history, economics, or foreign relations. By understanding the angle of the standard, you'll know what you should remember about the time period.

Now You Try It!

Read each question carefully and circle the number that goes with the answer choice you select.

1 **The struggle for control of the post–World War II world between American capitalism and Soviet communism is known as—**

    A Vietnam

    B the Cold War

    C containment

    D the domino theory

2 During the Yalta Conference in early 1945, President Franklin Roosevelt, Winston Churchill, and Joseph Stalin agreed to divide Germany into four zones, discussed the future of Eastern Europe, and—

F outlined the details of the Marshall Plan

G made a plan for offering economic aid to Japan

H made a plan for the structure of the United Nations

J formed the North Atlantic Treaty Organization (NATO)

3 To create a strong, democratic Western Europe while bolstering the U.S. economy, the United States extended massive monetary aid to Europe under the—

A Taft-Hartley Act

B Council for Mutual Economic Assistance

C Truman Doctrine

D Marshall Plan

4 What was the significance of the American-sponsored North Atlantic Treaty Organization (NATO) for Europe?

F It unified member nations by stating that an attack against one would be considered an attack against all.

G It was the first time that any European nation had joined a peacetime military alliance.

H It resulted in one common currency for all member nations.

J It provided the funds necessary to rebuild Western Europe after World War II and to give the United States a strong market for exports.

5 Because of the involvement of the United States in the Korean War—

A all of Korea was unified under a democratic government

B South Korea remained free of communist control

C China and the Soviet Union withdrew from Southeast Asia

D China joined the North Atlantic Treaty Organization (NATO)

6 **Why did the United States involve itself in the Korean and Vietnam wars?**

F   to defend nearby Japan, which had a very fragile postwar democracy

G   to stand up for human rights that were being threatened

H   to come to the aid of Korea and Vietnam, who were members of the North Atlantic Treaty Organization (NATO)

J   to continue its policy of containment by meeting instances of communist expansion in these nations with firm resistance

7 **What role did President Ronald Reagan play in bringing about the collapse of communism and the end of the Cold War?**

A   He undermined Soviet power in the world by giving huge amounts of economic aid to all nations that agreed not to trade with communist nations.

B   He stopped expanding the U.S. military and convinced the Soviet Union to do the same.

C   He directly supported the coup that overthrew the Soviet leadership.

D   He outspent the Soviet Union with a massive defense buildup, while meeting with Premier Gorbachev to warm relations and broker treaties.

8 **The destruction of the Berlin Wall came to symbolize—**

F   the end of the Cold War

G   American defeat in Vietnam

H   the effects of the Marshall Plan

J   the beginning of the Bosnian War

LESSON 11
THE CIVIL RIGHTS MOVEMENT

VIRGINIA AND UNITED STATES HISTORY SOL VUS.13 A,B "THE STUDENT WILL DEMONSTRATE KNOWLEDGE OF THE CIVIL RIGHTS MOVEMENT OF THE 1950S AND 1960S BY
- IDENTIFYING THE IMPORTANCE OF THE *BROWN V. BOARD OF EDUCATION* DECISION, THE ROLES OF THURGOOD MARSHALL AND OLIVER HILL, AND HOW VIRGINIA RESPONDED;
- DESCRIBING THE IMPORTANCE OF THE NATIONAL ASSOCIATION FOR THE ADVANCEMENT OF COLORED PEOPLE (NAACP), THE 1963 MARCH ON WASHINGTON, THE CIVIL RIGHTS ACT OF 1964, AND THE VOTING RIGHTS ACT OF 1965."

What This Means

The Civil Rights movement of the 1950s and 1960s was a crucial turning point for American race relations. After the Civil War, the promise of equality had, in the eyes of many people on both sides of the racial divide, stalled. Although slavery was abolished and universal voting rights were theoretically secured, African Americans were still regulated into a second-class citizenship through a policy of segregation. The standards above require you to be familiar with the *Brown v. Board of Education* Supreme Court case. You should also be familiar with Thurgood Marshall, who argued *Brown v. Board of Education* before the Supreme Court, and Oliver Hill, a lawyer who challenged school racism in his home state of Virginia. In addition, you should understand the importance of several main events of the movement including the March on Washington (the occasion of Martin Luther King Jr.'s famous "I have a dream" speech), the Civil Rights Act of 1964, and the Voting Rights Act of 1965. Finally, you should understand the role of the National Association for the Advancement of Colored People (NAACP) in the movement.

Sample

▶ **Why was the *Brown v. Board of Education* (1954) decision important to the Civil Rights movement at large?**

A It made it legal for a African American child to attend an all-white school.

B It held that it was illegal to pay African Americans a lower wage than would be paid to whites doing the same work.

C It struck down the legality of Jim Crow "separate but equal" laws, setting a precedent for African American–white integration.

D It established the legality of affirmative action programs in the United States.

How to Answer

To answer this question, you'll have to identify the principle that was addressed in the court case. *Brown v. Board of Education* involved the question of whether or not separate facilities for African American citizens were really equal. In this case, the facilities in question were public schools. Thurgood Marshall was an NAACP lawyer who argued that separate facilities were inherently unequal. He convinced the courts to overturn the earlier *Plessy v. Ferguson* decision, which had established the legality of "separate but equal."

Although the case of *Brown v. Board of Education* was ostensibly about the right of an African American student to attend school with white students, it had much larger implications for the Civil Rights movement. The case served as the first step in a decades-long process of integration and the attainment of true equal rights for African Americans.

Now that you have reviewed some details about the *Brown* case, look for the answer choice that best explains why it was so significant to the Civil Rights movement.

Answer choice **A** is "It made it legal for an African American child to attend an all-white school." *Brown v. Board of Education* did make it legal for an African American student to attend a white school, so this answer seems like a good choice. However, it doesn't speak to the implications for the Civil Rights movement at large, so it's a good idea to consider the other answer choices to see if there might be a better answer.

Answer choice **B** is "It held that it was illegal to pay African Americans a lower wage than would be paid to whites doing the same work." *Brown v. Board of Education* was not about equal pay for equal work; it was about the legality of the "separate but equal" doctrine. Therefore, **B** can be eliminated.

Answer choice **C** is "It struck down the legality of Jim Crow 'separate but equal' laws, setting a precedent for African American–white integration." *Brown v. Board of Education* did strike down the legality of the "separate but equal" doctrine and begin the process of African American–white integration. This answer choice is accurate and speaks to the importance of the case for the movement at large. Before you select this one, however, read the last choice.

Answer choice **D** is "It established the legality of affirmative action programs in the United States." *Brown v. Board of Education* did not address affirmative action programs; in fact, this issue would not enter public debate at all in the 1950s. Therefore, this answer choice can be eliminated. Now that you have considered all of the choices, you should know that **C** is correct.

Tip!

Sometimes multiple-choice questions ask you to think beyond straight facts and consider the meaning or implication of certain historical events. In the sample question, you need to know how the Supreme Court case *Brown vs. Board of Education* affected the Civil Rights movement. It isn't enough just to remember the outcome of the case. When you get a question that asks for the meaning or impact of an event, take a minute to think beyond straight facts. Look for an answer choice that mentions precedents or effects of the event.

Now You Try It!

Read each question carefully and circle the number that goes with the answer choice you select.

1   **What role did Thurgood Marshall play in the *Brown v. Board of Education* (1954) Supreme Court case?**

A   He was the consensus-builder in the Court who managed to get all of the justices to agree to the ruling.

B   He was the NAACP lawyer who convinced the Court that separate facilities for African Americans were inherently unequal.

C   He paid the legal costs for the plaintiff to bring the case against the Board of Education.

D   He was in charge of the federal troops sent to Little Rock to oversee the integration of a public high school.

2   **Who successfully litigated one of the school desegregation cases later decided by the Supreme Court in *Brown v. Board of Education*, thereby playing a key role in overturning the "separate but equal" doctrine?**

F   Martin Luther King Jr.

G   President Dwight Eisenhower

H   Earl Warren

J   Oliver Hill

3 **How did Virginia react to the ruling in the *Brown v. Board of Education* case?**

  A The board of supervisors in a Virginia county voted to close its schools rather than comply with desegregation.

  B Virginia lead the nation in desegregation of its public schools, completing the task in less than two years.

  C Violent protests broke out in several parts of the state following the 1954 ruling.

  D Parents kept their children home from school for one semester following early attempts to comply with the court-ordered desegregation.

4 **The National Association for the Advancement of Colored People (NAACP) played an important role in the Civil Rights movement *primarily* by—**

  F mobilizing the funds, strategies, and leaders necessary to advance the Civil Rights movement in the court system and beyond

  G serving as a labor union for African American workers in order to obtain higher wages and equality in the workplace

  H recruiting white citizens to help with advance the Civil Rights movement

  J organizing grassroots civil disobedience such as sit-ins and freedom rides

5 **What did the Civil Rights Act of 1964 accomplish?**

  A It outlawed the poll tax and literacy tests in polling places.

  B It put a significant amount of federal funds into programs designed to help African Americans living below the poverty line.

  C It implemented affirmative action programs in university admissions and government employment.

  D It forbade segregation in public places and outlawed discrimination by businesses and labor unions.

6 The ____ removed literacy tests and placed registration and voting processes under federal supervision.

F Fifteenth Amendment to the Constitution

G Civil Rights Act of 1964

H Voting Rights Act of 1965

J National Association for the Advancement of Colored People (NAACP)

7 Martin Luther King Jr.'s famous "I have a dream" speech was given—

A to members of the National Association for the Advancement of Colored People (NAACP)

B at the 1963 March on Washington

C from a Birmingham jail cell

D during the *Brown v. Board of Education* trial

8 Which of the following is true about the 1963 March on Washington?

F It was a highly visible event attended by thousands of people.

G It culminated in a violent outburst.

H It was a small gathering attended only by leaders of the Civil Rights movement.

J It was a gathering of all African American citizens.

LESSON 12
THE CONTEMPORARY UNITED STATES

VIRGINIA AND UNITED STATES HISTORY SOL VUS.14 "THE STUDENT WILL DEMONSTRATE KNOWLEDGE OF ECONOMIC, SOCIAL, CULTURAL, AND POLITICAL DEVELOPMENTS IN THE CONTEMPORARY UNITED STATES BY

- ANALYZING THE EFFECTS OF INCREASED PARTICIPATION OF WOMEN IN THE LABOR FORCE;
- ANALYZING HOW CHANGING PATTERNS OF IMMIGRATION AFFECT THE DIVERSITY OF THE UNITED STATES POPULATION, THE REASONS NEW IMMIGRANTS CHOOSE TO COME TO THIS COUNTRY, AND THEIR CONTRIBUTIONS TO CONTEMPORARY AMERICA;
- EXPLAINING THE MEDIA INFLUENCE ON CONTEMPORARY AMERICAN CULTURE AND HOW SCIENTIFIC AND TECHNOLOGICAL ADVANCES AFFECT THE WORKPLACE, HEALTH CARE, AND EDUCATION."

What This Means

This standard requires you understand some of the key historical factors that shaped the way you live today. One of the historical trends you must understand is the increasing diversity of the American workforce. As you learned in Lesson 9, women entered the workforce in great numbers during the Second World War. Although many of these women returned to domestic situations immediately after the war, an ever-increasing number of women chose to remain in the workplace instead of returning home. This increasing diversity in the workplace was mirrored by an increasing ethnic diversity in the population. Throughout the twentieth century, immigration from Europe, the traditional source of American immigrants, decreased. In their place, increasing numbers of immigrants from Asia, Africa, and South America came to the United States. Finally, you should understand how advances in technology have impacted all aspects of American life. As the United States entered the information age, new developments in communication revolutionized the way Americans work, play, and learn.

Sample

▶ **What principle was established by the landmark U.S. Supreme Court decision *Roe v. Wade* in 1973?**

A Abortion is legal under the constitutionally protected right to privacy.

B Abortion laws are in the legal domain of the individual states.

C Hospitals cannot refuse care to uninsured patients.

D Employers must provide maternity leave to new parents.

How to Answer

To answer this question, you'll have to identify the principle that was first addressed in the *Roe v. Wade* case. *Roe v. Wade* was a case involving a woman's right to choose to have an abortion. Norma McCorvey, a pregnant woman from Dallas, Texas, first challenged the constitutionality of a Texas abortion law. Using the pseudonym "Jane Roe," McCorvey sued Dallas County district attorney Henry Wade to be allowed to have an abortion.

The case went to the Supreme Court in 1971. Justice Harry A. Blackmun wrote the Court's majority opinion, the written document that announces the Court's decision and explains its reasoning. Blackmun stressed the need to resolve the issue of abortion based on an interpretation of the Constitution. A woman's right to privacy became a central argument in favor of legalizing abortion.

Now that you have reviewed the details of the *Roe v. Wade* case, select the choice that best represents the principle it addressed.

Answer choice **A** is "Abortion is legal under the constitutionally protected right to privacy." *Roe v. Wade* was a case involving a woman's right to have an abortion. One of the central arguments in the case was that this procedure fell under a citizen's right to privacy, making government involvement unconstitutional. This answer seems like a good choice, but you should check out the other answer choices before you select this one.

Answer choice **B** is "Abortion laws are in the legal domain of the individual states." *Roe v. Wade* did deal with state laws regarding abortion, so this answer might seem like a good choice. However, the case overturned state laws banning abortion. Therefore, it's clear that **A** is better, and this choice should be eliminated.

Answer choice **C** is "Hospitals cannot refuse care to uninsured patients." This case did not involve the issue of uninsured hospital patients. Therefore, **C** should be eliminated.

Answer choice **D** is "Employers must provide maternity leave to new parents." *Roe v. Wade* did not deal with employee benefits or the rights of new parents. Therefore, this answer choice should be eliminated. Now that you've considered all of the answer choices, you should know that **A** is correct.

Tip!

Some questions on the SOL exam ask about events that are still being debated today, so you've probably read about them in the newspaper or heard people talking about them. For example, the sample question about *Roe v. Wade*, which was decided in the 1970s, is still being talked about today because abortion is such a hot political issue. Try to identify recent events mentioned in the SOL exam and recall what you learned about them as they were happening.

Now You Try It!

Read each question carefully and circle the number that goes with the answer choice you select.

1 **In dealing with conflicts in Southeast Asia, presidents from Harry Truman to Richard Nixon made military decisions—**

A in cooperation with leaders of the North Atlantic Treaty Organization (NATO)

B in cooperation with the United Nations

C after securing the support of Congress

D largely without the consent of Congress

2 **The Twenty-sixth Amendment, which was ratified in 1971—**

F raised the drinking age to twenty-one

G lowered the voting age to eighteen

H limited the number of terms a president can serve

J loosened restrictions placed on immigration into the United States

3 **The "stagflation" of the 1970s was a combination of—**

A economic slowdown and inflation brought on by dependence on imports including oil

B high taxes and inflation brought on by uncertainty about the Cold War

C economic slowdown and deflation brought on by the high cost of the long Vietnam war

D currency (dollar) devaluation brought on by strong exporting markets in Japan and Europe

4 **What role did the media play in the resignation of President Richard Nixon during the Watergate scandal?**

F Television reporters aided government investigators by locating the incriminating taped White House conversations.

G A film about the events surrounding the scandal was instrumental in convincing leaders in Congress to take action against the president.

H Reporters at the *Washington Post* kept the story of the break-in and cover-up in the national spotlight with the help of a White House informer.

J Op-ed columnists at several prominent newspapers swayed public opinion against President Nixon.

5 **When President Ronald Reagan cut taxes without trimming the government budget, he instituted an enduring policy of—**

A wealth redistribution

B demand-side economics

C laissez-faire

D deficit spending

6 **What is the *main* reason Hispanic and Asian immigrants began to come to the United States in large numbers in the 1980s?**

F to escape communism

G to find economic opportunities

H to enjoy religious freedom

J to avoid military service

7 **What is one negative implication of scientific and technological breakthroughs in the area of health care?**

A Health care and health insurance has become increasingly expensive.

B People are not living as long.

C The health care industry does not employ as many people as it used to.

D The health care industry is no longer profitable.

8

Immigration by Continent of Residence

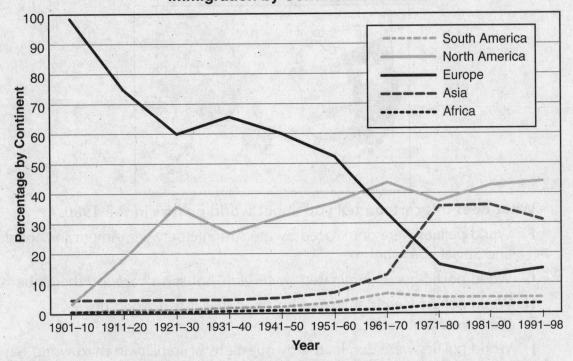

According to the graph above, which of the following statements is true about immigration to the United States in the 1970s and 1980s?

F The number of immigrants from Asia decreased as the number of immigrants from Europe increased.

G The number of immigrants from Africa sharply increased as the number of immigrants from North American decreased.

H The number of immigrants from Europe decreased as the number of immigrants from Asia increased.

J The number of immigrants from Asia decreased and the number of immigrants from North America decreased.

9 How has the Internet changed the workplace in the United States?

A It has lead to the employment of more women.

B Working from home or other remote locations has become more common.

C It has cut the profitability of many manufacturing businesses.

D It has lead to the employment of more minorities.

10

The World According to Reagan

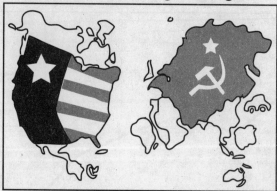

What does this cartoon tell you about world politics in the 1980s?

F   World politics were dominated by the struggle between American capitalism and Soviet communism.

G   World politics were dominated by several "hot spots" around the globe.

H   World politics were dominated by an unchallenged world power, the United States.

J   World politics were dominated by questions of stability in third world regions like Africa and South America.

REVIEW 3
LESSONS 10–12

1

■ NATO Countries　■ Warsaw Pact Countries

What do the nations in light gray represent?

A all the members of the United Nations

B Council for Mutual Economic Assistance (COMECON)

C World War II allies

D North Atlantic Treaty Organization (NATO)

2 The _____ held that any country falling to communism could topple its neighbors, leading to military engagement in Korea and Vietnam.

F domino theory

G military-industrial complex

H Warsaw Pact

J brinkmanship theory

3 What is the "crippled generation"?

A Those supporters of Reverend Martin Luther King Jr. and Robert Kennedy who were shaken by the assassination of both men.

B The Birmingham students who were injured as a result of Bull Connor's attacks on their peaceful march with fire hoses and police dogs.

C African American students who were forced to attend segregated schools.

D The students who were denied education for five years as a result of leaders' decision to close some of Virginia's schools in response to the order to integrate.

4 Why was the struggle for control of the postwar world between the United States and the Soviet Union referred to as the Cold War?

F because the bitter feelings between the antagonists lasted long after the war was over

G because no lives were lost as a result

H because it consisted of diplomatic struggles, skirmishes, and high-risk confrontations instead of direct military battles

J all the above

5 What social movement was sparked by the publication of Rachel Carson's book *Silent Spring* and the energy crisis of the 1970s?

A the environmental movement

B the counterculture movement

C the multicultural movement

D the isolationist movement

6 The National Organization of Women (NOW), formed in 1966, and other feminist groups lobbied in the 1960s and 1970s for—

F the right for women to vote and own property

G nationally funded universal health care

H gender equality in employment, salary, and access to higher education

J progressive goals including shorter workdays, child labor laws, and election reform

7 Why was the 1963 March on Washington important to the Civil Rights movement?

A The Civil Rights Act was passed as a direct result.

B The movement was made visible and mainstream.

C Reverend Martin Luther King Jr. emerged as a leader in the movement after this event.

D The Voting Rights Act was passed in Congress.

LESSON 13
THE INFLUENCE OF EUROPEAN ECONOMICS ON THE COLONIES

> **VIRGINIA AND UNITED STATES HISTORY SOL VUS.3** "THE STUDENT WILL DESCRIBE HOW THE VALUES AND INSTITUTIONS OF EUROPEAN ECONOMIC LIFE TOOK ROOT IN THE COLONIES AND HOW SLAVERY RESHAPED EUROPEAN AND AFRICAN LIFE IN THE AMERICAS."

What This Means

The United States began as European colonies. As such, the economic needs and institutions of the major European powers dominated the existence of the early colonies. You are expected to understand how European economic policies shaped the colonies. Slavery, possibly the most vexing and longest lasting legacy of colonial economic policy, continued well past the colonial era and had a profound impact on Americans of all races. You should be familiar with the slave trade and its long-term effects. Finally, because this standard is focused on economics, you should think about topics such as how work got done, how products were bought and sold, and how profits were made.

Sample

▶ **How was the English settlement Jamestown funded when it was founded in 1607?**

A One man, Sir Walter Raleigh, provided the necessary funding.

B The settlers raised money for the new colony by promising the king they would bring back gold and other fine materials from the rich New World.

C It was a proprietorship, meaning it was a gift of land given to the leaders of the Jamestown expedition by the king.

D The investors in the Virginia Company, who paid for the right to settle the colony, funded it.

How to Answer

To answer this question, you need to understand a common practice of the time, the joint-stock company. Two examples of joint-stock companies were the Virginia Company (which eventually gave the powerful state its name) and the Dutch East India Company. The Virginia Company consisted of a group of wealthy investors who paid the king for the right to settle in the New World, thereby beginning Jamestown. Although the king did not technically own the land, Jamestown began as a joint-stock company and eventually survived because of the help of the American Indians (First Americans) and the profitable tobacco crop.

Now that you have reviewed some details of the economic roots of Jamestown, look for the answer choice that best matches what you know.

Answer choice **A** is "One man, Sir Walter Raleigh, provided the necessary funding." Sir Walter Raleigh provided funding for the failed colony on Roanoke Island prior to the Jamestown expedition. Therefore, this answer choice can be eliminated.

Answer choice **B** is "The settlers raised money for the new colony by promising the king they would bring back gold and other fine materials from the rich New World." This answer might seem like a good choice because many Europeans believed in the riches of the New World after the Spanish conquistadors found the Aztec and Incan empires. However, no promise of gold was made by the Jamestown settlers. This answer choice can be eliminated.

Answer choice **C** is "It was a proprietorship, meaning it was a gift of land given to the leaders of the Jamestown expedition by the king." It was common for the king to grant colonial land to individuals in the 1600s; in fact, this is how many colonies got their start. Jamestown, however, was not a proprietorship, so this answer choice can be eliminated.

Answer choice **D** is "The investors in the Virginia Company, who paid for the right to settle the colony, funded it." Jamestown was funded by a group of wealthy Britons. They paid the king and were part of a joint-stock company. Now that you have read all the answer choices, you should know that **D** is correct.

When you look for the correct answer to a multiple-choice question, it is important to read all of the answer choices. If one or two of the choices contains words or phrases you are not familiar with, don't automatically eliminate them. For example, answer **C** in the sample question mentions "proprietorship." You might not know what a "proprietorship" is, but the meaning of the term is given. By using all the information, you should be able to choose correctly.

Now You Try It!

Read each question carefully and circle the number that goes with the answer choice you select.

1 **Spain believed in the economic policy of** *mercantilism*, **which meant that—**

   A the value of money goes down while the prices of goods move upward

   B American Indian families and towns were granted by the Spanish king to settlers to labor on farms

   C they felt it was their duty to convert the native people of North and South America to Catholicism

   D its colonies were to sell to and buy only from the mother country

2 **Why did the institution of slavery flourish more in the southern colonies such as Virginia and South Carolina than it did in the North?**

   F Northern colonies had outlawed slavery early in the seventeenth century.

   G Southern colonists were cultivating crops like tobacco that required intense labor.

   H Northern colonists were very religious and opposed to slavery on moral grounds.

   J Southern colonists came from parts of Europe that had slaves and had simply brought them along.

3 **Who did Virginia tobacco plantation owners turn to for labor before the use of African slaves?**

   A They used indentured servants.

   B They paid American Indians.

   C They farmed the land themselves.

   D They used convicts from England.

4 How did slavery hurt the development of southern colonies' economies?

F Too much capital was being spent on the costly transport of African slaves.

G Several potential trading partners in Europe decided to boycott colonies that used slaves.

H Constant slave revolts were costly and destructive.

J Many relied on cash crops and failed to develop cities as strong and diverse as those in the North.

5 Economically speaking, European settlers changed the Americas by creating a—

A surplus of available workers in the colonies

B complex economy with capital surpluses, specialized skills, and dependence on trade

C protectionist economy in which the colonies could trade only with other colonies

D subsistence-level farming economy

6 What was the *primary* economic activity ensuring the survival of *most* European settlers in the Americas in the seventeenth and eighteenth centuries?

F factory work

G farming

H building

J hunting

7 Slave "acculturation" was the process African slaves used to—

 A establish a community and culture of their own in the Americas

 B establish their own businesses and currency in the Americas

 C reunite separated families

 D escape from slave owners

8 How did currency change in the Americas due to the arrival of European settlers?

 F Paper money was no longer used after the arrival of the Europeans.

 G Luxury items such as jewelry became a common currency.

 H Paper money and coins took the place of objects or food.

 J Food items became a common currency.

9

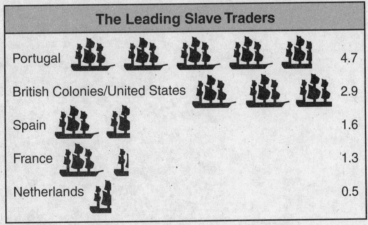

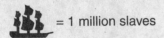 = 1 million slaves

According to this chart, who were the leading slave traders?

 A British

 B Spanish

 C French

 D Portuguese

10

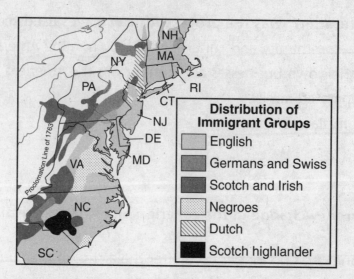

Distribution of
Immigrant Groups

English

Germans and Swiss

Scotch and Irish

Negroes

Dutch

Scotch highlander

According to this map, which European country had the most settlers in the thirteen colonies in 1770?

F France

G England

H Germany

J Holland

LESSON 14
GEOGRAPHY AND ECONOMICS
FROM 1800 THROUGH 1850

VIRGINIA AND UNITED STATES HISTORY SOL VUS.6 A,C "THE STUDENT
WILL DEMONSTRATE KNOWLEDGE OF THE MAJOR EVENTS DURING THE FIRST HALF OF THE NINETEENTH
CENTURY BY
- IDENTIFYING THE ECONOMIC, POLITICAL, AND GEOGRAPHIC FACTORS THAT LED TO TERRITORIAL
  EXPANSION AND ITS IMPACT ON THE AMERICAN INDIANS (FIRST AMERICANS);
- DESCRIBING THE CULTURAL, ECONOMIC, AND POLITICAL ISSUES THAT DIVIDED THE NATION,
  INCLUDING SLAVERY, THE ABOLITIONIST AND WOMEN'S SUFFRAGE MOVEMENTS, AND THE ROLE
  OF THE STATES IN THE UNION."

What This Means

You are expected to understand the major economic and geographic issues of the
first half of the nineteenth century. To do this, you should consider how products
were manufactured and how profits were made. Think about how the country
pushed westward and how this affected American Indians. Finally, you should be
familiar with major political issues of the day such as slavery, the movement to
abolish slavery, the states' rights debate, and women's suffrage (the right to vote).

Sample

▶ **How did the ruling in the 1819 Supreme Court case *McCulloch v. Maryland*
set a precedent for the relationship between the states and the Union?**

  A The ruling extended the Bill of Rights to state governments.

  B The ruling asserted that states did not have the power to tax the national
     bank, showing that national law is more powerful than state law.

  C The ruling asserted that states could write their own constitutions.

  D The ruling made it legal for states to nullify national laws, a right exercised
     by South Carolina during the presidency of Andrew Jackson.

How to Answer

To answer this question, you'll have to identify the principle that was first addressed
in the *McCulloch* case and then think about how this principle affected the power
balance between states and the federal government (the Union). *McCulloch v.
Maryland* was a case involving the state of Maryland's attempt to tax the Second
National Bank. The Court, under Chief Justice John Marshall, ruled that Maryland was
barred from this action, thereby asserting that federal law was supreme over state law.

This ruling was an important milestone in defining the relationship between the states and the federal government, as it clearly gave the balance of power to the federal government. This was a balance that many state leaders, particularly in the South, did not like. It would continue to be an incendiary issue until the Civil War settled it once and for all.

Now that you have reviewed the details and implications of the *McCulloch v. Maryland* case, look for an answer choice that explains the precedent explained in the previous paragraph.

Answer choice **A** is "The ruling extended the Bill of Rights to state governments." *McCulloch v. Maryland* was about the right of a state to tax the national bank and had little to do with the Bill of Rights. Eliminate this answer choice.

Answer choice **B** is "The ruling asserted that states did not have the power to tax the national bank, showing that national law is more powerful than state law." Maryland tried to levy taxes on the Second National Bank. It was barred from doing so by this ruling, which clearly set a precedent that national law was more powerful than state law. This answer looks like a good choice, but you should check the other choices before you select this one.

Answer choice **C** is "The ruling asserted that states could write their own constitutions." This case was not about the right of states to write their own constitutions, nor does this answer choice speak to the relationship of states to the union. **B** is a better option.

Answer choice **D** is "The ruling made it legal for states to nullify national laws, a right exercised by South Carolina during the presidency of Andrew Jackson." Actually, in the *McCulloch* case, the Supreme Court ruled that national law was more powerful than state law. Now that you have considered all of the answer choices, you should know that **B** is correct.

It might be useful for you to keep in mind the time period the question refers to. In the sample question, you are given the year 1819, which means the question deals with early American history. You should be able to eliminate the choice about Andrew Jackson and the Nullification Crisis right away because you know that event comes a little later. You can also eliminate the choice about extending the Bill of Rights to the states, because this action didn't occur until the Fourteenth Amendment was passed after the Civil War.

Now You Try It!

Read each question carefully and circle the number that goes with the answer choice you select.

1 The Jefferson administration acquired _____ from France in 1803, doubling the geographic size of the United States.

    A the Alaska Territory

    B Texas

    C the Louisiana Territory

    D the Great Lakes

2 What economic factor(s) led to the settlement of frontier land for the creation of cotton plantations?

    F The frontier land was affordable and fertile.

    G There was massive European demand for cotton.

    H A mechanical invention, the cotton gin, made processing faster.

    J all of the above

3 How did westward expansion of the United States affect the American Indians?

    A They were forced off land their land or killed.

    B They integrated with the new settlers and became farmers.

    C They moved to eastern cities to work in new industries.

    D They were enslaved on the new cotton plantations.

4 How did the slavery issue make admitting new states into the Union difficult during the first half of the nineteenth century?

    F All new states were kept neutral on the issue of slavery.

    G All new states had to pledge to be slave states in order to enter the Union.

    H Leaders tried to maintain an even balance of slave states and free states.

    J All new states had to pledge to be free states in order to enter the Union.

5 What political movement began in earnest with a convention in Seneca Falls, New York, in 1848?

A the Civil Rights movement

B the women's suffrage movement

C the abolitionist movement

D the prohibition movement

6 What was the major difference between the economy in the North and the economy in the South during the mid-nineteenth century?

F The North was industrial, while the economy of the South was agricultural and based on one product.

G The economy of the North was agricultural, while the South was based on technology.

H The South ran a diversified economy, while the North relied on the exportation of just one product.

J The northern economy depended on small farms, while the southern economy depended on small factories.

7 _____ drew parallels between slavery and women's rights issues, claiming women in the nineteenth cetnury were often trapped in "domestic slavery."

A Margaret Sanger

B Elizabeth Cady Stanton

C Frederick Douglass

D Sarah and Angelina Grimke

8 How did William Lloyd Garrison further the goals of the abolitionist movement?

F He published the weekly abolitionist paper *The Liberator* and founded the American Anti-Slavery Society.

G He planned and organized the first abolitionist rally at Seneca Falls in New York.

H He started a violent slave rebellion in the fields of Virginia and died a martyr for the cause of abolition.

J He wrote *Uncle Tom's Cabin*, which convinced many Americans to join the abolitionist movement.

9

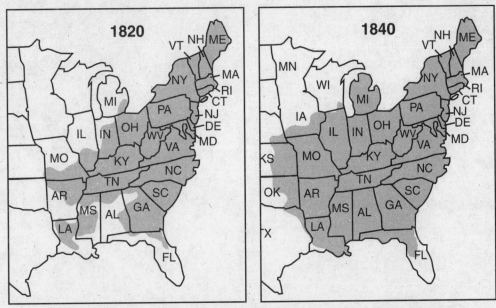

The shaded areas show areas of American settlement.

What does the shading on these two maps reveal about the American population during the first half of the nineteenth century?

A The population pushed into new frontier territory, shifting to the west.

B The population migrated north and into the largest cities.

C The population pushed closer to the East Coast.

D The population migrated in large numbers to southern states.

LESSON 15
THE U.S. ECONOMY FROM RECONSTRUCTION THROUGH THE EARLY TWENTIETH CENTURY

VIRGINIA AND UNITED STATES HISTORY SOL VUS 8 B "THE STUDENT WILL DEMONSTRATE KNOWLEDGE OF HOW THE NATION GREW AND CHANGED FROM THE END OF RECONSTRUCTION THROUGH THE EARLY TWENTIETH CENTURY BY DESCRIBING THE TRANSFORMATION OF THE AMERICAN ECONOMY FROM A PRIMARILY AGRARIAN TO A MODERN INDUSTRIAL ECONOMY AND IDENTIFYING MAJOR INVENTIONS THAT IMPROVED LIFE IN THE UNITED STATES."

What This Means

The period of history from the end of Reconstruction to the turn of the twentieth century was one of rapid change and growth. You are expected to be familiar with the sweeping economic and cultural changes that were characteristic of this period. You should understand how the United States switched from an economy built on farming to one built on industry and manufacturing. Much of this shift was technology driven, and you should be able to identify the major technological inventions of the era.

Sample

▶ **How did the way in which businesses were operated change during the era following Reconstruction?**

   A They went from small, owner-operated enterprises to large government-run conglomerates.

   B Businesses went from being highly regulated by state governments to being free of restriction in a renewal of laissez-faire policy.

   C Businesses could no longer be passed down from parents to children.

   D They went from small, owner-operated enterprises to corporations in which the company became a legal entity separate from its owner.

How to Answer

To answer this question, you'll have to identify how American businesses were changing during the period following Reconstruction. After the Civil War, the United States entered a period of rapid industrialization. Although this evolution had begun before the war (and even tipped the scales in favor of the North), the true shift from an agrarian to an industrial society occurred after the Reconstruction Era. Businesses went from being small, owner operated enterprises to corporations in which the company was a legal entity separate from its owner(s). This setup allowed owners to sell stock and offer limited liability to the new owner-investors. These new corporations grew quickly and were largely unregulated by the government.

Now that you have reviewed some details of the shift in businesses models during this time period, look for the answer that best explains what happened.

Answer choice **A** is "They went from small, owner-operated enterprises to large government-run conglomerates." It's true that businesses started out as small, owner-operated enterprises prior to the shift mentioned in this question. However, the U.S. government did not start taking these small businesses over. Therefore, this answer choice can be eliminated.

Answer choice **B** is "Businesses went from being highly regulated by state governments to being free of restriction in a renewal of laissez-faire policy." Laissez-faire policy did come into play during this era, as businesses enjoyed a climate in which they were free of regulation. This choice should be eliminated, however, because they did not start out being highly regulated by state government, and this answer choice doesn't speak to a change in the way businesses were operated.

Answer choice **C** "Businesses could no longer be passed down from parents to children." The practice of passing down the family business continued during this period and through the present. Therefore, this answer choice must be eliminated.

Answer choice **D** is "They went from small, owner-operated enterprises to corporations in which the company became a legal entity separate from its owner." During this era, businesses did switch from small, owner-operated proprietorships to corporations in which owners could sell stock. You know that, as a result, businesses grew rapidly. This answer looks like a good choice. Now that you have considered all of the choices, you should know that **D** is correct.

Sometimes it is helpful to think about what you know about a subject before you answer the history question associated with it. For example, you probably know something about how businesses are run in the United States. The sample question asks you how their operation changed after Reconstruction, so chances are the way they are run today might be relevant. Sometimes even though a policy or a way of doing things evolved a long time ago, it is the same to this day.

Now You Try It !

Read each question carefully and circle the number that goes with the answer choice you select.

1 **From the end of Reconstruction through the early twentieth century, the American economy transformed from primarily agrarian to—**

   A service-based

   B communist

   C socialist

   D industrial

2 **What happened in the era after Reconstruction as a result of the shift from small, owner-operated businesses to corporations?**

   F Industry grew rapidly.

   G Monopolies started to develop.

   H Wealth became increasingly concentrated in the hands of a few affluent Americans.

   J all of the above

3 **Because of the growth of industry during the era between Reconstruction and the early twentieth century, people moved in large numbers to—**

   A cities

   B rural areas

   C the South

   D suburbs

4 **Which of the following changes in the workplace could *best* be attributed to Alexander Graham Bell's major invention?**

   F slower communication time between employees

   G decreases in employee salaries

   H increased coordination between distant offices

   J high levels of quality control for factories

5 Which invention, developed by Thomas Edison in 1879, allowed people to work longer hours?

A   the phonograph

B   the incandescent lightbulb

C   the electric trolley

D   the kerosene lantern

6

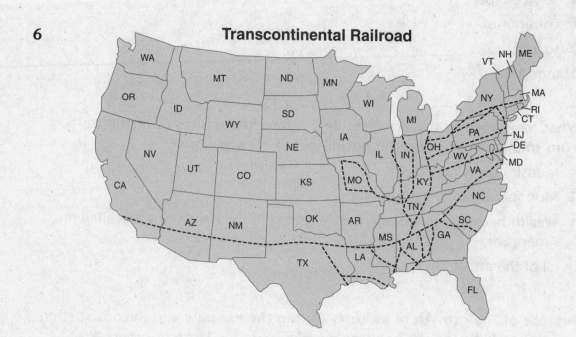

Transcontinental Railroad

Why were rail lines like the ones shown here so important to industrial expansion?

F   They opened up Canadian markets to East Coast merchants.

G   They made transcontinental transport cheap and efficient.

H   They slowed the pace of western expansion and kept customers on the East Coast.

J   all of the above

7 **What does the term *laissez-faire* mean in the context of economics?**

A It refers to the government policy of changing base interest rates to smooth out the cyclical nature of the economy.

B It refers to a business arrangement in which owners agree to fix prices and/ or divide territory so that there is no competition.

C It refers to a "hands off" policy in which the government allows business to operate without regulation.

D all the above

8 **Industrialists, like John Pierpont "J.P." Morgan, who wielded enormous power and made money through ruthless business practices, were known as—**

F robber barons

G muckrakers

H Populists

J Know-Nothings

LESSON 16
THE UNITED STATES AFTER 1890

VIRGINIA AND UNITED STATES HISTORY SOL VUS.9 A,C "THE STUDENT WILL DEMONSTRATE KNOWLEDGE OF THE EMERGING ROLE OF THE UNITED STATES IN WORLD AFFAIRS AND KEY DOMESTIC EVENTS AFTER 1890 BY
- EXPLAINING THE CHANGING POLICIES OF THE UNITED STATES TOWARD LATIN AMERICA AND ASIA AND THE GROWING INFLUENCE OF THE UNITED STATES IN FOREIGN MARKETS;
- EXPLAINING THE CAUSES OF THE GREAT DEPRESSION, ITS IMPACT ON THE AMERICAN PEOPLE, AND THE WAYS THE NEW DEAL ADDRESSED IT."

What This Means

In the late nineteenth century and early twentieth century, the United States entered an imperialistic phase of expansion. This expansion started with the successful war against Spain, which gave the United States control of Spain's Latin American and Asian territories. The construction of the Panama Canal is a lasting legacy of this period, as are the continued tensions between the United States and its southern neighbors. You are expected to know how the United States interacted with Latin America and Asia in the era after 1890. As the United States spread its economic and military influence abroad, the nation entered an era of economic prosperity and speculation. These good times, which reached a peak in the "Roaring Twenties," came to a sudden and catastrophic end in the late 1920s. The resulting economic depression and its effects are known as the Great Depression. You need to understand the impact of the Great Depression, its affect on the American people, and the New Deal policies enacted in response.

Sample

▶ **How did "dollar diplomacy" dictate American foreign policy in Latin America during the early twentieth century?**

A It held that economic interests would guide military intervention in the region, forcing neighbors to be friendly to American businesses.

B It held that the United States would pay neighbors in Latin America to cooperate with American goals.

C It was a policy in which the United States declared it would consolidate the economies of several Latin American countries with its own, thereby making the U.S. dollar the currency of the entire region.

D It was a policy in which the United States demanded "open door" access to trade in the region.

How to Answer

To answer this question, you'll have to be familiar with U.S. attitudes toward Latin America at this time. Prior to the policy of "dollar diplomacy," Presidents Monroe and Roosevelt declared that Latin America was the domain of the United States. The United States, said President Theodore Roosevelt, would act as police in the region. President William Howard Taft (1908–1912) continued this policy when he coined the phrase "dollar diplomacy," but he made it more clearly about economics, asserting that U.S. military intervention would be guided directly by American economic interests. As a result, marines were sent to keep order in neighboring nations and keep them friendly to U.S. business interests. During this time, the United States took over economic control of Cuba, the Dominican Republic, Haiti, and Nicaragua.

Now that you have reviewed the main idea behind "dollar diplomacy," look for an answer choice that best explains how the policy shaped U.S. actions in Latin America during the early twentieth century.

Answer choice **A** is "It held that economic interests would guide military intervention in the region, forcing neighbors to be friendly to American businesses." President Taft said that economic interests would shape military engagement in the region when he coined the term "dollar diplomacy," so this looks like a good choice. You should check out the other answer choices, though, before you select this one.

Answer choice **B** is "It held that the United States would pay neighbors in Latin America to cooperate with American goals." This answer might seem like a good choice because it fits with the term "dollar diplomacy," but you know that the United States often got involved militarily in the region during this time. Because **A** is more accurate, this choice can be eliminated.

Answer choice **C** is "It was a policy in which the United States declared it would consolidate the economies of several Latin American countries with its own, thereby making the U.S. dollar the currency of the entire region." The United States never made its dollar the universal currency of Latin America, so this answer choice can be eliminated.

Answer choice **D** is "It was a policy in which the United States demanded 'open door' access to trade in the region." The United States always had access to trade in Latin America; it didn't have to demand it. This answer choice can be eliminated. Now that you have considered all of the answer choices, you should know that **A** is correct.

Tip!

If a multiple-choice question includes a phrase that you are unsure of, think about the words outside of a historical context. For example, you may not know exactly what "dollar diplomacy" means, but you can probably guess that it had something to do with money or economics interests. Just by thinking about this, you can eliminate **D** because it does not mention money or economics.

Now You Try It!

Read each question carefully and circle the number that goes with the answer choice you select.

1 **Why did the United States send marines to keep order in several Latin American countries during the early twentieth century (1908–1917)?**

   A The United States was aiding Latin American nations trying to gain their independence from European colonial powers.

   B It was a "dollar diplomacy" effort to keep the region stable for U.S. economic interests.

   C It was part of the United States' attempt to gain "open door" entry into closed economic markets.

   D The United States was worried about the spread of communism in the region.

2 **How did the United States implement its Open Door policy toward Chinese markets?**

   F Secretary of State John Hay sent a letter to the European powers demanding an "open door" to Chinese trade.

   G U.S. Marines were sent to the region.

   H The United States began trading with Chinese neighbors in Asia.

   J President William Howard Taft negotiated trade agreements with the Chinese government, securing an "open door" for U.S. business interests.

3 As evidenced by the Spanish-American War, in which the United States gained control of the Philippines, Guam, and Puerto Rico, the turn of the century was a time in which American foreign policy was—

A bilateral

B neutral

C isolationist

D expansionist

4 What practice in large part caused the stock market crash of 1929, sparking the Great Depression of the 1930s?

F accumulating a combination of stocks, bonds, and land investments

G buying stocks on the margin by paying only a fraction of their cost

H the practice of buying one stock and selling it the same day

J the practice of banks investing their deposits in the stock market

5 The _____ was a New Deal employment program in which roads, public housing, and sewers were built.

A Agricultural Adjustment Act

B Federal Deposit Insurance Corporation

C Public Works Administration

D Securities and Exchange Commission

6 Because banks and a small number of industrialists were the stock market's primary investors, the crash of ____ caused widespread unemployment and bank failure, sparking the Great Depression.

F 1929

G 1927

H 1931

J 1941

Use the following chart to answer questions 7 and 8.

Act or Program	Acronym	Year Enacted	Significance
Civil Works Administration	CWA	1933	Provided public works jobs at fifteen dollars per week to four million workers in 1934.
Civilian Conservation Corps	CCC	1933	Sent 250,000 young men to work camps to perform reforestation and conservation tasks. Removed surplus of workers from cities, provided healthy conditions for boys, and provided money for families.
Federal Emergency Relief Act	FERA	1933	Distributed millions of dollars of direct aid to unemployed workers.
National Youth Administration	NYA	1935	Received $3.3 billion appropriation from Congress for public works projects.
Public Works Administration	PWA	1933	Provided part-time employment to more than two million high school and college students.
Securities and Exchange Commission	SEC	1934	Regulated stock market and restricted margin buying.
Social Security Administration	SSA	1935	Response to critics (Dr. Townsend and Huey Long). Provided pensions, unemployment insurance, and aid to blind, deaf, disabled, and dependent children.
Tennessee Valley Authority	TVA	1933	Federal government built series of dams to prevent flooding and sell electricity. First public competition with private power industries.
Works Progress Administration	WPA	1935	Employed 8.5 million workers in construction and other jobs, but more importantly provided work in arts, theater, and literary projects.

7 **The Securities and Exchange Commission, formed in 1934—**

A regulated stock market and restricted margin buying

B insured bank deposits

C provided work in arts, theater, and literary projects

D distributed millions of dollars of direct aid to unemployed workers

8 **Which New Deal program hired men to build a series of dams to prevent flooding and to sell electricity in Appalachia?**

F National Youth Administration

G Federal Emergency Relief Act

H Tennessee Valley Authority

J Social Security Act

LESSON 17
CIVICS

VIRGINIA AND UNITED STATES HISTORY SOL VUS.4 AND VUS.5 "THE STUDENT WILL DEMONSTRATE KNOWLEDGE OF EVENTS AND ISSUES OF THE REVOLUTIONARY PERIOD BY
- ANALYZING HOW THE POLITICAL IDEAS OF JOHN LOCKE AND THOSE EXPRESSED IN *COMMON SENSE* HELPED SHAPE THE DECLARATION OF INDEPENDENCE.

"THE STUDENT WILL DEMONSTRATE KNOWLEDGE OF THE ISSUES INVOLVED IN THE CREATION AND RATIFICATION OF THE UNITED STATES CONSTITUTION AND HOW THE PRINCIPLES OF LIMITED GOVERNMENT, CONSENT OF THE GOVERNED, AND THE SOCIAL CONTRACT ARE EMBODIED IN IT BY
- EXPLAINING THE ORIGINS OF THE CONSTITUTION, INCLUDING THE ARTICLES OF CONFEDERATION;
- IDENTIFYING THE MAJOR COMPROMISES NECESSARY TO PRODUCE THE CONSTITUTION, AND THE ROLES OF JAMES MADISON AND GEORGE WASHINGTON;
- EXAMINING THE SIGNIFICANCE OF THE VIRGINIA DECLARATION OF RIGHTS AND THE VIRGINIA STATUTE FOR RELIGIOUS FREEDOM IN THE FRAMING OF THE BILL OF RIGHTS."

What This Means

These standards are all about the Declaration of Independence and the U.S. Constitution, the two cornerstone documents of American democracy. Thomas Jefferson, author of the Declaration of Independence, and James Madison, chief architect behind the Constitution, were educated and informed citizens, familiar with the important political and philosophical thought of their day. You are expected to understand how the Declaration of Independence was shaped by the ideas of philosopher John Locke and *Common Sense*, the influential pamphlet by Thomas Paine. The SOL may test you on the content and context of the Constitution. To be fully prepared, you should be familiar with the principles outlined in the U.S. Constitution as well as the major controversies and compromises that shaped it. You must understand the role of Virginians James Madison and George Washington in the creation and ratification of the Constitution. Finally, you should understand the significance of the Virginia Declaration of Rights and the Virginia Statute for Religious Freedom, both of which contributed to the development of the Bill of Rights.

Sample

▶ **How did the publication of Thomas Paine's *Common Sense* contribute to the creation of the Declaration of Independence?**

A The pamphlet contained a list of all the taxes placed on the colonies by the British and articulated the popular "no taxation without representation" slogan for the first time.

B The pamphlet was widely circulated in the colonies and encouraged ratification of the U.S. Constitution.

C The popular pamphlet argued in favor of independence and offered a solid case for the merits of a republican government over a monarchy.

D The pamphlet argued in favor of colonial independence and presented a solid case for the merits of separation of church and state.

How to Answer

To answer this question, you need to be familiar with the content of Paine's *Common Sense* and its impact on the colonists. The pamphlet was published in 1775 and widely circulated in the thirteen colonies. It proved even more popular than an earlier pamphlet by James Otis called *The Rights of the British Colonies Asserted and Proved* (1765), which argued against taxation without representation. *Common Sense* argued in favor of colonial independence from Great Britain and presented a case for the merits of a republican form of government (as opposed to a monarchy). This pamphlet helped to ignite support for the independence movement and provided some of the ideas presented in the Declaration of Independence the following year.

Now that you have reviewed some details of the content of Paine's *Common Sense*, look for an answer choice that best represents the ideas in the preceding paragraph.

Answer choice **A** is "The pamphlet contained a list of all the taxes placed on the colonies by the British and articulated the popular 'no taxation without representation' slogan for the first time." The "no taxation without representation" credo was coined by James Otis in his pamphlet ten years before the publication of *Common Sense*. Therefore, this answer choice can be eliminated.

Answer choice **B** is "The pamphlet was widely circulated in the colonies and encouraged ratification of the U.S. Constitution." Although it is true that the pamphlet was widely circulated in colonies, it did not encourage ratification of the U.S. Constitution, which wouldn't be written for another twelve years. *The Federalist Papers* did encourage ratification; therefore, this answer choice can be eliminated.

Answer choice **C** is "The popular pamphlet argued in favor of independence and offered a solid case for the merits of a republican government over a monarchy." *Common Sense* did argue in favor of independence, which inflated the ranks of the patriots. In addition, it offered a case for republican government, which provided some raw material for the ideas expressed in the Declaration of Independence. This answer seems like a good choice, but you should check out all of the choices before you select this one.

Answer choice **D** is "The pamphlet argued in favor of colonial independence and presented a solid case for the merits of separation of church and state." It is true that the pamphlet argued in favor of colonial independence, but it did not address the issue of separation of church and state. Because **C** is a better answer, this choice can be eliminated. Now that you have considered all of the choices, you know that **C** is correct.

Remember when you read over answer choices that, in order for a choice to be correct, *all* of its parts must be correct. Even if a selection is partially true, it might be the wrong answer. Use caution and reread your selection to be sure of its validity before you move on to the next question. For example, consider the choice "The pamphlet argued in favor of colonial independence and presented a solid case for the merits of separation of church and state" in the sample question. The first part of the statement is true: *Common Sense* did argue in favor of colonial independence. However, the merits of separation of church and state are not its main idea. There is a better answer choice available.

Now You Try It!

Read each question carefully and circle the number that goes with the answer choice you select.

1 The U.S. Constitution was written to replace—

   A the Articles of Confederation

   B the Declaration of Independence

   C the Bill of Rights

   D the Rights of the British Colonies Asserted and Proved

2 In what way did the political ideas of John Locke contribute to the creation of the Declaration of Independence?

    F He established the principle of checks and balances, a major component of the U.S. Constitution.

    G He suggested that the rule of monarchy is inherently corrupt because it places too much power in the hands of one person.

    H He was an anarchist who advocated throwing off the rule of government at any opportunity.

    J He suggested that government should rest on popular consent and that rebellion is permissible when government doesn't serve the purpose for which it is established.

3 How did the Articles of Confederation *most* significantly differ from the U.S. Constitution?

    A They made no provisions for states' rights.

    B They established a very weak central government.

    C They strictly regulated trade with foreign nations.

    D They were never sent to the states for approval.

4 What role did James Madison play in the development of the U.S. Constitution?

    F He suggested the Great Compromise, which established two houses of Congress.

    G He chaired the Constitutional Convention in Philadelphia in 1787.

    H He wrote portions of the document and played a large role in getting it ratified.

    J He asserted the need for a bill of rights prior to ratification.

5 Fifty-five delegates from twelve states convened in Philadelphia in 1787 for the Constitutional Convention, choosing _____ to chair the convention.

    A Benjamin Franklin

    B James Madison

    C Thomas Jefferson

    D George Washington

6 To solve the problem of how to fairly represent all states in the legislature, the Great Compromise was agreed upon, thereby—

F establishing two bodies of Congress

G counting each slave as three-fifths of a person

H creating three branches of government with checks and balances

J setting term limits for all government leader positions

7

Ratification of the Constitution

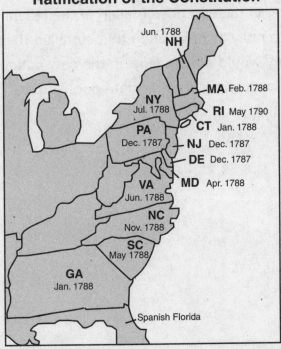

What does this map suggest about the process of ratifying the U.S. Constitution?

A Some states never ratified the Constitution.

B It was a process that took a couple months to complete.

C Southern states were the slowest to ratify the new Constitution.

D It was a challenging process that took several years to complete.

8 **The Virginia Declaration of Rights and the Virginia Statute for Religious Freedom both served as models for—**

   F the Articles of Confederation

   G the Bill of Rights

   H the Declaration of Independence

   J the U.S. Constitution

9 **The Three-Fifths Compromise solved the issue of—**

   A too much power in the executive branch of the federal government

   B getting states to ratify a constitution that curtailed their rights

   C how long slavery would remain legal in the new nation

   D how to count slaves when figuring state populations

REVIEW 4
LESSONS 13–17

1 In what way in the eighteenth century did the economic system in the southern colonies differ from the economic system in Europe?

    A It was largely dependent upon slave labor.

    B It was driven mainly by larger scale manufacturing.

    C It consisted solely of subsistence farming.

    D It was highly diversified in product output.

2 The massacre of 850 American Indians (First Americans) and their removal from Illinois by federal troops occurred with the support of the Jackson administration during—

    F the War of 1812

    G the Blackhawk War

    H the Mexican-American War

    J the Nullification Crisis

3 With his weekly newspaper, *The Liberator*, William Lloyd Garrison advanced the cause of—

    A women's suffrage

    B segregation

    C abolition

    D all of the above

4 One of the chief effects of the invention of the automobile was—

    F a population movement out of urban centers into the suburbs

    G decreased production of fossil fuels such as oil

    H increased pressure on lawmakers to pass Prohibition legislation

    J a return to an agriculture-based economy in the southern states

5 Why was the period following Reconstruction one of rapid industrialization for the United States?

    A The laissez-faire policies of the government encouraged rapid expansion of industry.

    B Large labor pools were made available to industrialists as a result of a flood of European immigrants.

    C The Civil War promoted the growth of industry and demonstrated the usefulness of railroads and telegraphs.

    D all of the above

6 What were "Hoovervilles" during the Great Depression?

F pockets of the country that supported President Hoover

G deserted towns filled with foreclosed businesses

H government-sponsored work camps

J clusters of makeshift homes

7 What ultimately pulled the United States out of the Great Depression?

A Great Society programs and immigrants

B German disarmament at the end of World War I

C New Deal programs and World War II

D loans from European countries

8 _____ helped to convince the Founding Fathers that the Articles of Confederation needed to be replaced in favor of a stronger federal government.

F The Townshend Acts

G Shays's Rebellion

H The Whiskey Rebellion

J The Nullification Crisis

ANSWER KEY FOR
LESSONS AND REVIEWS

Lesson 1

Sample A

1 C
2 J
3 B
4 G
5 A
6 F
7 D
8 H
9 A

Lesson 2

Sample B

1 A
2 G
3 D
4 H
5 A
6 G
7 C
8 H
9 B
10 F

Lesson 3

Sample A

1 C
2 F
3 B
4 J
5 C
6 F
7 D
8 G
9 A

Lesson 4

Sample **D**

1 **C**
2 **J**
3 **A**
4 **J**
5 **C**
6 **G**
7 **A**
8 **G**
9 **A**

Lesson 5

Sample **C**

1 **A**
2 **H**
3 **D**
4 **F**
5 **B**
6 **H**
7 **D**
8 **F**
9 **C**

Review 1

1 **B**
2 **F**
3 **C**
4 **F**
5 **B**
6 **J**
7 **A**
8 **H**

Lesson 6

Sample **B**

1   **A**
2   **H**
3   **A**
4   **G**
5   **D**
6   **F**
7   **A**
8   **H**
9   **A**

Lesson 7

Sample **C**

1   **C**
2   **J**
3   **A**
4   **H**
5   **A**
6   **G**
7   **A**
8   **G**
9   **A**

Lesson 8

Sample **A**

1   **B**
2   **F**
3   **J**
4   **B**
5   **C**
6   **F**
7   **C**
8   **J**
9   **A**

Lesson 9

Sample D

1 A
2 G
3 D
4 H
5 A
6 J
7 B
8 J
9 B
10 H

Review 2

1 B
2 J
3 B
4 J
5 A
6 H
7 D

Lesson 10

Sample B

1 B
2 H
3 D
4 F
5 B
6 J
7 D
8 F

Lesson 11

Sample C

1 B

2 J

3 A

4 F

5 D

6 H

7 B

8 F

Lesson 12

Sample A

1 D

2 G

3 A

4 H

5 D

6 G

7 A

8 H

9 B

10 F

Review 3

1 D

2 F

3 D

4 H

5 A

6 H

7 B

Lesson 13

Sample D

1	D
2	G
3	A
4	J
5	B
6	G
7	A
8	H
9	D
10	G

Lesson 14

Sample B

1	C
2	J
3	A
4	H
5	B
6	F
7	D
8	F
9	A

Lesson 15

Sample D

1	D
2	J
3	A
4	H
5	B
6	G
7	C
8	F

Lesson 16

Sample A

1 B

2 F

3 D

4 G

5 C

6 F

7 A

8 H

Lesson 17

Sample C

1 A

2 J

3 B

4 H

5 D

6 F

7 D

8 G

9 D

Review 4

1 A

2 G

3 C

4 F

5 D

6 J

7 C

8 G

THE PRACTICE TESTS

HOW TO TAKE THE PRACTICE TESTS

By this point you've made it through the lessons in the book, which cover the standards tested on the Virginia Standards of Learning (SOL) End of Course Virginia and United States History Assessment. Congratulations! Now it's time to try your hand at a practice Virginia and United States History SOL test. There are two in this section.

Each practice Virginia and U.S. History SOL test includes seventy multiple-choice questions, just like the real test. An answer sheet comes before each practice test. Tear or cut out the answer sheet, and answer your questions on the practice test by filling in the bubbles accordingly. Use a No. 2 pencil, and take each practice test just as if you were taking the actual test. That means you should sit at a desk and avoid interruptions. Turn off the television, stereo, and even the telephone.

The Virginia and U.S. History SOL test is untimed, so you'll have as much time as you'll need to complete the test. However, you should still take the test in one sitting because you won't be allowed to take a break during the real Virginia and U.S. History SOL test.

When you've completed the first practice test, check the answers and explanations on pages 211–226. Make sure to read through the explanations to all the questions—even the ones you got right. The explanations can help you figure out different ways to approach certain questions. After taking the first practice test and checking your answers, take a break. (We do not recommend taking both practice tests in the same day. Give your brain time to rest!) The answers and explanations for the second practice test can be found on pages 227–238.

When you're ready, cut out the answer sheet and get started on the first practice test. Good luck!

PRACTICE TEST 1 ANSWER SHEET

Name: _____

1. (A) (B) (C) (D)
2. (F) (G) (H) (J)
3. (A) (B) (C) (D)
4. (F) (G) (H) (J)
5. (A) (B) (C) (D)
6. (F) (G) (H) (J)
7. (A) (B) (C) (D)
8. (F) (G) (H) (J)
9. (A) (B) (C) (D)
10. (F) (G) (H) (J)
11. (A) (B) (C) (D)
12. (F) (G) (H) (J)
13. (A) (B) (C) (D)
14. (F) (G) (H) (J)
15. (A) (B) (C) (D)
16. (F) (G) (H) (J)
17. (A) (B) (C) (D)
18. (F) (G) (H) (J)
19. (A) (B) (C) (D)
20. (F) (G) (H) (J)
21. (A) (B) (C) (D)
22. (F) (G) (H) (J)
23. (A) (B) (C) (D)

24. (F) (G) (H) (J)
25. (A) (B) (C) (D)
26. (F) (G) (H) (J)
27. (A) (B) (C) (D)
28. (F) (G) (H) (J)
29. (A) (B) (C) (D)
30. (F) (G) (H) (J)
31. (A) (B) (C) (D)
32. (F) (G) (H) (J)
33. (A) (B) (C) (D)
34. (F) (G) (H) (J)
35. (A) (B) (C) (D)
36. (F) (G) (H) (J)
37. (A) (B) (C) (D)
38. (F) (G) (H) (J)
39. (A) (B) (C) (D)
40. (F) (G) (H) (J)
41. (A) (B) (C) (D)
42. (F) (G) (H) (J)
43. (A) (B) (C) (D)
44. (F) (G) (H) (J)
45. (A) (B) (C) (D)
46. (F) (G) (H) (J)

47. (A) (B) (C) (D)
48. (F) (G) (H) (J)
49. (A) (B) (C) (D)
50. (F) (G) (H) (J)
51. (A) (B) (C) (D)
52. (F) (G) (H) (J)
53. (A) (B) (C) (D)
54. (F) (G) (H) (J)
55. (A) (B) (C) (D)
56. (F) (G) (H) (J)
57. (A) (B) (C) (D)
58. (F) (G) (H) (J)
59. (A) (B) (C) (D)
60. (F) (G) (H) (J)
61. (A) (B) (C) (D)
62. (F) (G) (H) (J)
63. (A) (B) (C) (D)
64. (F) (G) (H) (J)
65. (A) (B) (C) (D)
66. (F) (G) (H) (J)
67. (A) (B) (C) (D)
68. (F) (G) (H) (J)
69. (A) (B) (C) (D)
70. (F) (G) (H) (J)

PRACTICE TEST 1

1 To address concerns that the Constitution failed to safeguard individual liberties, supporters of the Constitution promised the passage of—

   A the Articles of Confederation

   B the Bill of Rights

   C the Fourteenth Amendment

   D the Nineteenth Amendment

2 All of the following are true of the Democratic-Republican Party *except* that it—

   F was founded in opposition to the Federalist Party

   G was led by Thomas Jefferson and James Madison

   H split because of controversy over the "corrupt bargain"

   J was the party of Abraham Lincoln

3 ┌─────────────────────────────────┐
   │ **AIMS OF THE GREAT SOCIETY**   │
   │   │
   │ 1. Eradicate racial injustice │
   │ 2. Share abundance   │
   │ 3. Overcome disease   │
   │ 4. Dispel ignorance   │
   └─────────────────────────────────┘

   The Civil Rights Acts of 1964 and the Voting Rights Act of 1965 are examples of Great Society legislation addressing—

   A Aim 1

   B Aim 2

   C Aim 3

   D Aim 4

4 Which of the following was the largest and *most* active group of colonists who supported independence from Britain?

   F the Sons of Liberty

   G the Iroquois Nation

   H the Tories

   J the Federalists

5 Which of the following important American patriots was *not* from Virginia?

   A George Washington

   B Thomas Jefferson

   C James Madison

   D Alexander Hamilton

6 The sweeping legislative agenda that President Franklin D. Roosevelt proposed to aid Americans during the Great Depression was called—

   F the Fair Deal

   G the New Deal

   H the Square Deal

   J the Great Society

Go On

7

Eastern Europeans

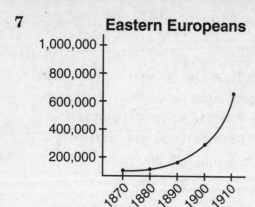

Northern Europeans

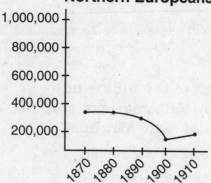

According to the graphs representing this forty-year period—

A the number of European immigrants to the United States decreased

B the number of European immigrants to the United States went up and down

C the number of Danish immigrants to the United States increased

D the number of European immigrants to the United States increased dramatically

8 **Which of the following Constitutional amendments signified the success of the suffrage movement?**

F Fourth Amendment, forbidding unreasonable searches

G Sixteenth Amendment, permitting a national income tax

H Nineteenth Amendment, enfranchising women

J Twenty-first Amendment, repealing Prohibition

9 **Which of the following would *most* likely have contributed to job reductions in the U.S. automotive industry?**

A increased American use of public transportation

B decreased demand for automobiles in the United States

C increased use of computers and robots in automobile manufacturing

D increased availability of jobs in other industries

10 **Which of the following Supreme Court decisions established the principle of judicial review?**

F *Marbury v. Madison*

G *McCulloch v. Maryland*

H *Dred Scott v. Sandford*

J *Brown v. Board of Education of Topeka, Kansas*

11 Which of the following is *best* described as a rebellion by American Indians (First Americans) against British colonists who were expanding into the western frontier?

A King Philip's War

B the French and Indian War

C the Stono Uprising

D the Trail of Tears

12

Writer P:	I wrote *The Grapes of Wrath,* a 1939 novel dramatizing the dust bowl.
Writer Q:	I wrote *The Jungle,* a 1906 novel about exploitation in the meat-packing industry.
Writer R:	I wrote *The Great Gatsby,* a 1925 novel depicting the new American lifestyle of the 1920s.
Writer S:	I wrote *The Sound and the Fury,* a 1929 novel illustrating life in the rural south

Of the writers above, the only one who would be considered a muckraker is—

F Writer P

G Writer Q

H Writer R

J Writer S

13 After the Boston Tea Party, the British closed Boston Harbor with which of the following acts of Parliament?

A the Navigation Acts

B the Proclamation of 1763

C the Townshend Acts

D the Coercive Acts

14 A major weakness of the Articles of Confederation was the—

F high federal taxes

G lack of a central executive power

H repression by a strong federal government

J excessive presidential powers

15

> "The only trouble about this town is that it is too large. You cannot accomplish anything in the way of business, you cannot even pay a friendly call, without wasting a whole day to it."
>
> —*Mark Twain, complaining about New York City, 1867*

Which of the following innovations did the *most* to rectify Twain's complaint?

A the telephone

B the phonograph

C the telegraph

D the lightning rod

Go On ⇨

16 The forced journey of slaves from Africa to the New World was called—

F seasoning

G the Stono Uprising

H the Dark Journey

J the Middle Passage

17 U.S. Unemployment 1915–1942

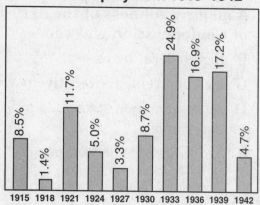

According to the graph, unemployment in the United States—

A steadily decreased between 1915 and 1942

B was a result of the U.S. trade deficit

C generally decreased after the 1933 beginning of the New Deal

D drove Americans back to the farm between 1915 and 1942

18

What does this illustration of Columbus's landing in the Americas suggest about the first interaction between Europeans and American Indians?

F The two cultures were similar.

G It was an ambush.

H It was a friendly exchange.

J It was a violent meeting.

19 Which U.S. president pioneered the "spoils system," whereby government appointments are rewarded to supporters who are owed favors?

A Thomas Jefferson

B Andrew Jackson

C Abraham Lincoln

D Theodore Roosevelt

20

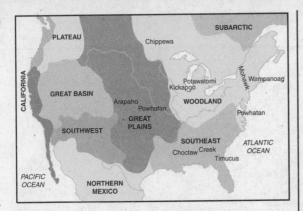

Use the map above and your knowledge of European settlement of the Americas to choose which American Indian tribe the English Jamestown settlers interacted with the *most*.

F Wampanoag

G Timucua

H Mohawk

J Powhatan

21 Which of the following issues is *most* associated with the women's rights movement after World War II?

A welfare reform

B campaign finance reform

C minimum wage legislation

D equal employment opportunities

22 The mid-nineteenth century belief that the United States was destined and obligated to control as much territory in North America as possible was referred to as—

F manifest destiny

G the Monroe Doctrine

H mercantilism

J the Marshall Plan

23 The famous colonial rabble-rouser who wrote the convincing pro-independence pamphlet *Common Sense* was—

A Thomas Paine

B Patrick Henry

C Samuel Adams

D John Jay

Go On

Use these maps to answer questions 24 and 25.

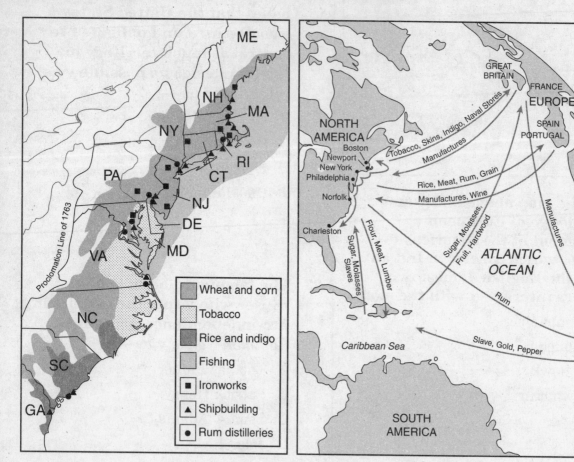

24 Which American colonies were exporting tobacco to Europe in the eighteenth century?

  F North Carolina, Virginia, Maryland

  G New York, Pennsylvania

  H South Carolina, Rhode Island, Delaware

  J Massachusetts, Connecticut

25 What products were shipped from Europe to the American colonies and Africa in the eighteenth century?

  A tobacco

  B sugar and rum

  C manufactured goods

  D meat and grain

26

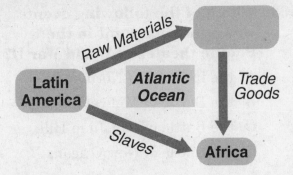

In the eighteenth-century trade triangle above, which continent belongs in the blank rectangle?

F South America

G Asia

H North America

J Europe

27 Migration within the United States from rural areas to urban areas was *mainly* the result of which of the following?

A foreign immigration

B increased urban crime

C increased industrialization

D reduced soil quality

28

Which sentence *best* summarizes the main point of the cartoon above?

F The Supreme Court and Congress worked together in conceiving the New Deal.

G The Supreme Court and President Franklin D. Roosevelt worked together in conceiving the New Deal.

H The Supreme Court kept the New Deal from succeeding.

J The Supreme Court struck down many pieces of New Deal legislation, while approving others.

29 Which of the following of Thomas Jefferson's actions represented a vast departure from his philosophy of strict construction?

A authorship of the Virginia Statute on Religious Freedom

B opposition to the First Bank of the United States

C support for the Virginia and Kentucky Resolutions

D the Louisiana Purchase

Go On

30 World War I saw the introduction of all of the following dangerous new weapons *except*—

F the machine gun

G nuclear submarines

H fighter planes

J poison gas

31 Which of the following was *not* a major contributor to the dust bowl of the 1930s?

A sustained drought

B removal of natural vegetation

C abandonment of farms by people moving west

D overfarming of land to meet increased demand during World War I

32 The 1950s construction of the Eisenhower interstate system reflected an unprecedented American reliance upon—

F railroads

G automobiles

H buses

J airplanes

33 Which of the following events was a turning point in the Pacific theater of World War II?

A the invasion of Normandy

B the Battle of Midway

C the Battle of San Juan Hill

D the Battle of New Orleans

34 Alexander Graham Bell, who spent much of his life working to improve the lives of the deaf, revolutionized business and personal communications with what 1876 invention?

F the phonograph

G the telegraph

H the incandescent lightbulb

J the telephone

35 The Virginia and Kentucky Resolutions, written by James Madison and Thomas Jefferson, asserted states' rights and opposed what federal policy?

A the Monroe Doctrine

B the creation of the First Bank of the United States

C the Alien and Sedition Acts

D westward expansion

36 The United States bought Florida from—

F France

G Britain

H Mexico

J Spain

37

> "A policy of isolation did well enough when we were an embryo nation. But today things are different.... We are 65 million people, the most advanced and powerful on earth, and regard to our future welfare demands an abandonment of the doctrines of isolation."
>
> —*U.S. Senator Orville Platt, 1893*

Platt's words indicate that an important reason for expanded foreign policy was—

A colonial expansion

B economic expansion

C military expansion

D cultural expansion

38 Which of the following *best* describes U.S. involvement in the Korean War?

F U.S. involvement was part of a détente policy.

G U.S. involvement was an example of the policy of containment.

H The United States and the Soviet Union committed military forces to fight as allies in Korea.

J The United States did not commit military forces to fight in Korea.

39 All of the following are true of the Battle of New Orleans *except*—

A the British burned Washington, D.C., in revenge

B it was the final battle in the War of 1812

C it vaulted General Andrew Jackson to national fame

D the peace treaty ending the war was signed before the battle

40 The principle of popular sovereignty was enacted by which of these legislative agreements?

F the Missouri Compromise

G the annexation of Texas

H the Kansas-Nebraska Act

J the Fugitive Slave Act

Go On

41

The Ten Largest U.S. Cities by Population in 1870 and 1910

1870	1910
New York 942,292	New York 4,766,883
Philadelphia 674,022	Chicago 2,185,283
Brooklyn* 419,921	Philadelphia 1,549,008
St. Louis 310,864	St. Louis 687,029
Chicago 298,977	Boston 670,585
Baltimore 267,354	Cleveland 560,663
Boston 250,526	Baltimore 558,485
Cincinnati 216,239	Pittsburgh 533,905
New Orleans 191,418	Detroit 465,766
San Francisco 149,473	Buffalo 523,715

* Brooklyn was consolidated into New York in 1898.
Source: U.S. Census Data

Which of the following was *most* responsible for the population trends shown in the chart above?

A growth of commercial centers

B improvements in agrarian techniques

C African American migration north

D increasing industrialization

42 Which of the following guarantees equal rights to all citizens and was ratified as a condition of the end of Reconstruction?

F Thirteenth Amendment

G Fourteenth Amendment

H Fifteenth Amendment

J Eighteenth Amendment

43

> In 1890, the federal government created Yosemite, Sequoia, and King's Canyon National Parks in California. As Los Angeles and San Francisco grew, the lack of available water suitable for drinking and irrigation became a major issue. In the first years of the twentieth century, Los Angeles constructed a 238-mile aqueduct to channel water from the Sierra Nevada to the city. In 1913, the federal government permitted a dam to be built in Hetch Hetchy, just north of Yosemite National Park, to provide water to San Francisco.

The incidents outlined above illustrate which of the following?

A federal interference in state affairs

B how conservationists limited growth in California

C the tension between the needs of growing urban areas and the movement to conserve natural resources

D the impact of urban pollution on the natural environment

44 All of the following were Cold War responses to Soviet aggression *except*—

F President Truman's decision to drop the atomic bomb

G the Berlin Airlift

H the North Atlantic Treaty Organization (NATO)

J the Truman Doctrine

45

Throughout the nineteenth and twentieth centuries, immigrants came to the United States for one primary reason. From the Irish immigrants who poured into the industrial North in the mid-nineteenth century to the Eastern European immigrants of the late nineteenth and early twentieth centuries and the Mexican and Latin American immigrants of the late twentieth century, the American Dream has always been the primary motivation.

The primary motivation to which the speaker refers is *best* explained as—

A California gold

B economic opportunity

C free education

D freedom of speech

46 The Supreme Court's decision in *McCulloch v. Maryland* established that—

F the Supreme Court has the right to strike down unconstitutional laws

G states have the right to nullify those federal laws that they dislike

H federal legislation is supreme and states cannot overrule it

J all prisoners must be read their rights upon arrest

47 Which of these colonial American documents outlines the "inalienable rights" of "life, liberty, and the pursuit of happiness"?

A *Common Sense*

B the Declaration of Independence

C the Constitution

D *The Federalist Papers*

48 Which of the following was a result of the Civil Rights movement?

F the election of John F. Kennedy as president

G the Twenty-fourth Amendment, eliminating the poll tax

H the end of the Ku Klux Klan

J the Twenty-sixth Amendment, lowering the voting age to eighteen

Go On →

49 Which of the following was the *least* important factor behind the construction of the Panama Canal?

A lower-cost transportation of goods from the East Coast to the West Coast

B greater naval mobility

C easier trade between the Southeast Asia and the East Coast

D profits from canal construction

50 Which of the following legislative acts did the *most* to increase voting among African Americans?

F Fourteenth Amendment

G Fifteenth Amendment

H Civil Rights Act of 1964

J Voting Rights Act of 1965

51 The tradition of serving as president for no more than two full terms was first established by—

A George Washington

B Thomas Jefferson

C James Madison

D Andrew Jackson

52 All of the following were major events of the Civil Rights movement *except*—

F Freedom Summer

G the founding of the Southern Christian Leadership Conference

H the Seneca Falls Convention

J the Montgomery bus boycott

53 Who was the immigrant and scientist who proposed the creation of the Manhattan Project, taught at Princeton University, and revolutionized physics with his theory of relativity?

A Thomas Edison

B Nicola Tesla

C Guglielmo Marconi

D Albert Einstein

54 The Nullification Crisis was precipitated by a disagreement between the Congress and the state of South Carolina on the—

F national tariff

G printing of currency

H size of the U.S. Army

J issue of slavery

55 Which of these Virginians is known as "the Father of the Constitution" because of his primary role in drafting the Constitution?

A Patrick Henry

B Thomas Jefferson

C James Madison

D George Washington

56 Which of the following is the *best* evaluation of the scope of job opportunities for women during World War II?

F very little change

G a severe limitation

H a vast expansion

J an expansion, but only within the armed forces

57 Henry Ford's invention of the assembly line allowed most Americans to afford a private automobile. Which of the following industries has expanded the *most* because of the widespread use of automobiles?

A forestry

B communications

C petroleum processing and refining

D publishing

58 In October 1929, the economy of the United States took a drastic downturn. In one day, "Black Tuesday," the value of stocks held by American investors fell from approximately $87 billion to about $55 billion.

The *most* immediate cause of this loss was—

F widespread unemployment

G bank failures in the United States

H the crash of the stock market

J the Great Depression

59 Which of the following events led *most* directly to U.S. involvement in World War II?

A the German invasion of Czechoslovakia

B the Cuban missile crisis

C the Japanese bombing of Pearl Harbor

D the assassination of Archduke Ferdinand

60 The earliest settlers in Massachusetts came from Great Britain seeking—

F profitable trade

G religious freedom

H cleaner air

J advanced farming tools

Go On

61 The groundbreaking book *The Souls of Black Folk* was written in 1903 by which important reformer?

A Susan B. Anthony

B W. E. B. Du Bois

C Martin Luther King Jr.

D Rosa Parks

62

U.S. Oil Consumption
(data in quadrillion BTU)

1910	1
1920	2.5
1930	5.0
1940	7.5
1950	12.5
1960	15.5
1970	29.0
1980	34.0

If the trend in the chart continues, environmentalists believe the *least* effective solution would be to—

F expand public transportation

G use coal to generate power

H improve solar energy efficiency

J increase use of electric automobiles

63 The first slaves introduced to the American colonies arrived in which state in 1619?

A Georgia

B Kentucky

C South Carolina

D Virginia

64 Which of the following foreign policy statements declared that the United States would not tolerate European interference in affairs in the Americas?

F the Monroe Doctrine

G the Tariff of Abominations

H the Good Neighbor policy

J the Open Door policy

65 Relocation of urban employees to the suburbs in the years after World War II was largely the result of the popularization of—

A computers

B automobiles

C telephones

D airplanes

66

> **PROVISIONS OF THE**
> **WAR POWERS RESOLUTION (1973)**
>
> President who commits troops to combat must present rationale to Congress within 48 hours;
>
> president needs congressional approval to deploy troops for 60 days or more;
>
> without congressional approval, president must withdraw troops;
>
> Congress can order troop withdrawal before 60 days have passed.

The War Powers Resolution was a response to concerns over—

F congressional abuse of authority in deployment of U.S. military forces

G underuse of U.S. military forces

H an imbalance of powers in deployment of U.S. military forces

J Supreme Court interference in the deployment of U.S. military forces

67

Major Legislation of the Great Society	Purpose of Legislation
Economic Opportunity Act (1964)	To inaugurate "War on Poverty" programs
"Medicare Act" (1965)	To provide government medical care for the elderly
Higher Education Act (1965)	To provide grants for student loans and university construction

Based on the legislation above, it is fair to conclude that the Great Society—

A attempted to expand the scope of government social programs

B introduced new regulations on businesses

C reduced the size of the federal government

D reversed many of the programs of the New Deal

Go On

68

"Our long national nightmare is over."

—President Gerald Ford, upon assuming the presidency after Richard Nixon's resignation on August 9, 1974

When Ford mentioned "our long national nightmare," he was referring to—

F American military intervention in Southeast Asia

G the Watergate scandal

H the McCarthy hearings

J the Great Depression

69

- • WRA Relocation Camp
- States with more than 1,000 Japanese residents

Which of the following conclusions does the map above *best* support?

A Most Japanese Americans lived on the West Coast in 1942.

B There were no Japanese Americans living in Nevada in 1942.

C There were three internment camps in New York.

D All of the internment camps were located on riverbanks.

70

PRESIDENT WOODROW WILSON'S FOURTEEN POINTS

1. Open covenants of peace
2. Absolute freedom of navigation
3. Removal of trade barriers
4. Reduction of arms to defensive levels
5. Impartial adjustment of all colonial claims
6. Evacuation of all foreign troops from Russia
7. Evacuation of all foreign troops from Belgium
8. Evacuation of all German troops from France; restoration of Alsace-Lorraine to France
9. Readjustment of Italy's borders
10. Self-determination for nationalities in Austria-Hungary
11. Evacuation of foreign troops from Romania, Serbia, and Montenegro
12. Self-determination for nationalities in the Turkish Empire
13. Establishment of an independent Poland
14. Establishment of a league of nations

Which of Wilson's Fourteen Points ultimately failed to pass the U.S. Senate?

F Point 2

G Point 4

H Point 5

J Point 14

PRACTICE TEST 2 ANSWER SHEET

Name: _____

1. (A) (B) (C) (D)
2. (F) (G) (H) (J)
3. (A) (B) (C) (D)
4. (F) (G) (H) (J)
5. (A) (B) (C) (D)
6. (F) (G) (H) (J)
7. (A) (B) (C) (D)
8. (F) (G) (H) (J)
9. (A) (B) (C) (D)
10. (F) (G) (H) (J)
11. (A) (B) (C) (D)
12. (F) (G) (H) (J)
13. (A) (B) (C) (D)
14. (F) (G) (H) (J)
15. (A) (B) (C) (D)
16. (F) (G) (H) (J)
17. (A) (B) (C) (D)
18. (F) (G) (H) (J)
19. (A) (B) (C) (D)
20. (F) (G) (H) (J)
21. (A) (B) (C) (D)
22. (F) (G) (H) (J)
23. (A) (B) (C) (D)

24. (F) (G) (H) (J)
25. (A) (B) (C) (D)
26. (F) (G) (H) (J)
27. (A) (B) (C) (D)
28. (F) (G) (H) (J)
29. (A) (B) (C) (D)
30. (F) (G) (H) (J)
31. (A) (B) (C) (D)
32. (F) (G) (H) (J)
33. (A) (B) (C) (D)
34. (F) (G) (H) (J)
35. (A) (B) (C) (D)
36. (F) (G) (H) (J)
37. (A) (B) (C) (D)
38. (F) (G) (H) (J)
39. (A) (B) (C) (D)
40. (F) (G) (H) (J)
41. (A) (B) (C) (D)
42. (F) (G) (H) (J)
43. (A) (B) (C) (D)
44. (F) (G) (H) (J)
45. (A) (B) (C) (D)
46. (F) (G) (H) (J)

47. (A) (B) (C) (D)
48. (F) (G) (H) (J)
49. (A) (B) (C) (D)
50. (F) (G) (H) (J)
51. (A) (B) (C) (D)
52. (F) (G) (H) (J)
53. (A) (B) (C) (D)
54. (F) (G) (H) (J)
55. (A) (B) (C) (D)
56. (F) (G) (H) (J)
57. (A) (B) (C) (D)
58. (F) (G) (H) (J)
59. (A) (B) (C) (D)
60. (F) (G) (H) (J)
61. (A) (B) (C) (D)
62. (F) (G) (H) (J)
63. (A) (B) (C) (D)
64. (F) (G) (H) (J)
65. (A) (B) (C) (D)
66. (F) (G) (H) (J)
67. (A) (B) (C) (D)
68. (F) (G) (H) (J.)
69. (A) (B) (C) (D)
70. (F) (G) (H) (J)

PRACTICE TEST 2

1 The Jamestown colony eventually succeeded because of which two factors?

A the help from the Powhatan Confederacy of American Indians and the decision to grow and export tobacco

B the help of slaves from Africa and the help of the Powhatan Confederacy of American Indians (First Americans)

C the location of the colony in a warm climate and the decision to grow and export sugar cane

D the continuous flow of new colonists from Great Britain and favorable weather conditions

2

What does the pamphlet above suggest about interactions between Europeans and American Indians?

F The two groups never spoke to each other.

G Some Europeans tried to understand the language of the American Indians.

H All Europeans forced American Indians to speak English.

J American Indians were not eager to interact with European settlers.

3 The migration of American Indian tribes to the west of the Mississippi River during the Jacksonian Era was due in large part to—

A the Taft-Hartley Act

B overfarming of land in the east

C the Indian Removal Act of 1830

D the Mexican-American War

4 How did federal banking policies change under President Andrew Jackson's leadership?

F The Second National Bank was dissolved.

G The Second National Bank was established.

H The government took a larger role in regulating the economy.

J The government put federal banks in each state in the Union.

5 Industrialists of the late 1800s contributed to economic growth by—

A supporting the efforts of labor unions

B establishing large corporations

C encouraging government ownership of banks

D opposing protective tariffs

Go On ⇒

6 How did slavery in the United States reshape the lives of African families trapped in this institution?

F Slavery helped to ensure that all African children would be educated.

G Slavery integrated black and white families into one extended unit.

H Slavery encouraged strong African family units and promoted marriage.

J Slavery broke up families as members were sold to different owners.

7

> "Gone, gone—sold and gone,
> To the rice-swamp dank and lone,
> Where the slave-whip ceaseless swings,
> Where noisome insect stings,
> Where the Fever Demon strews
> Poison with the falling dews,
> Where sickly sunbeams glare
> Through the hot and misty air,—
> Gone, gone—sold and gone,
> To the rice-swamp dank and lone,
> From Virginia's hills and waters,—
> Woe is me, my stolen daughters!"
>
> —John Greenleaf Whittier

The purpose of the nineteenth-century poem above is to convince American citizens to—

A support women's suffrage

B oppose women's suffrage

C support the abolition of slavery

D oppose the abolition of slavery

8 How did the Missouri Compromise deal with the divisive slavery issue as new states entered the Union?

F It preserved the balance of slave states and free states and set a boundary north of which slavery would be banned.

G It set a date for the abolition of slavery in all states west of the Mississippi River.

H It preserved the balance of slave states and free states by decreeing that states had to enter the Union in pairs.

J It preserved the balance of power between slave states and free states by creating two federal capitals.

9 Which Supreme Court ruling asserted the supremacy of federal law over state law, helping to clarify the role of states in the Union?

A *Griswold v. Connecticut*

B *Plessy v. Ferguson*

C *Marbury v. Madison*

D *McCulloch v. Maryland*

10 The first successful colony in Virginia, founded in 1607 and led by John Smith, was—

F Jamestown

G Richmond

H Raleigh

J Roanoke

11 Henry Ford revolutionized factories in all industries with his invention of the—

A assembly line

B steam engine

C railroad engine

D forty-hour work week

12

Which of the following *best* describes the main idea of the cartoon?

F The Treaty of Versailles treated Germany and Russia equally.

G Germany came out of World War I strong and proud.

H The Treaty of Versailles was a way for the Allied powers to help Germany rebuild.

J The Treaty of Versailles was a way for the Allied powers to punish Germany.

13 The spread of automobiles in the United States during the years following World War II resulted in—

A the growth of residential suburban communities for those Americans working in cities

B more people moving into urban areas

C the growth of rural farming communities

D increased demand for urban high-rise apartment buildings

14 Which of the following *most* contributed to the defeat of the Confederate States of America?

F strong support of European nations for the Union

G less support among the citizens of its states

H underdeveloped industrial infrastructure

J inferior military leadership

15 Elizabeth Cady Stanton, Susan B. Anthony, and Lucretia Mott are *most* closely associated with—

A the Civil Rights movement

B the suffrage movement

C the Communist Party

D the muckrakers

Go On

16 The Pilgrims lived within the framework of the Mayflower Compact after they landed at—

F Plymouth

G Salem

H Jamestown

J Philadelphia

17 The Civil Rights movement made momentous gains during the 1950s and 1960s using all of the following strategies *except*—

A court decisions

B legislative advances

C organized nonviolent civil disobedience

D armed insurrection

18 The Nullification Crisis was a showdown between President Andrew Jackson and the state of South Carolina over states' rights and the specific issue of—

F the Alien and Sedition Acts

G federal tariffs

H the Second National Bank

J the slave trade

19

1898

Hawaiian Islands

Philippines

Wake Island

Guam

Midway Islands

Which sentence *best* explains the general situation depicted in the cartoon?

A Congress intended for all of the U.S. possessions in the Pacific Ocean to become states.

B The United States had provoked the Spanish-American War by invading Guam.

C After the Spanish-American War the United States possessed an American empire in the Atlantic and Pacific oceans.

D The United States colonized many islands that had belonged to Japan.

20 The phrase "gold, God, and glory" *best* describes the motivations of which of the following groups during the age of discovery?

F conquistadors

G American Indians

H Pilgrims

J Puritans

21

U.S. Exports

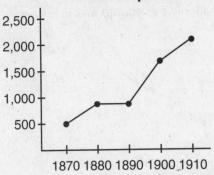

2,500
2,000
1,500
1,000
500

1870 1880 1890 1900 1910

U.S. Imports

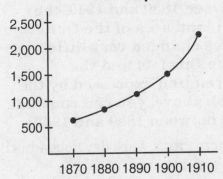

2,500
2,000
1,500
1,000
500

1870 1880 1890 1900 1910

According to the graphs above, between 1870 and 1910—

A the United States ran a consistent budget surplus

B the U.S. government increased in size

C the United States ran a consistent budget deficit

D U.S. exports increased more than U.S. imports

22 **The forced relocation of the Cherokee tribe from North Carolina to Oklahoma in the 1830s is known as—**

F the French and Indian War

G the Seminole War

H the Trail of Tears

J the Stono Uprising

23

> In a 1950 speech in Wheeling, West Virginia, a U.S. senator from Wisconsin said, "I have here in my hand a list of 205—a list of names that were made known to the secretary of state as members of the Communist Party and who nevertheless are still working and shaping policy in the state department."

Who was the politician who spoke the words above and led a congressional hearing into communist infiltration of the American government and society?

A Joseph McCarthy

B Henry Cabot Lodge

C Dwight D. Eisenhower

D Richard Nixon

Go On ⟹

24 Which of the following cases decided by the Supreme Court under the leadership of Chief Justice Earl Warren did the *most* to advance the goals of the Civil Rights movement?

F *Brown v. Board of Education of Topeka, Kansas*

G *Gideon v. Wainwright*

H *Griswold v. Connecticut*

J *Miranda v. Arizona*

25 Which of the following American military interventions was *not* based on the Cold War theory of containment?

A the Berlin Airlift

B the Cuban missile crisis

C the Persian Gulf War

D the Vietnam War

26 Which of the following contributed *most* to the acceleration of communications in the nineteenth century?

F the telegraph

G completion of the transcontinental railroad

H the popularization of electricity in cities

J the Pony Express

27 Population Density 1880–1940
(residents per square mile)

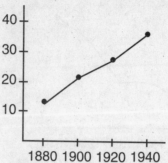

Source: U.S. Census Bureau

Between 1880 and 1940, the total land area of the United States changed very little. Given this fact and the information expressed by the graph above, you can conclude that between 1880 and 1940—

A more cities were developed in the United States

B immigration to the United States increased

C there was no more available land in the United States for farming

D the U.S. population grew

28 Which of the following Cold War events was an example of détente?

F the Berlin Airlift

G the Cuban missile crisis

H the Korean War

J Nixon's visit to China

29 The separation of church and state is an important element in all of the following documents *except*—

A the Mayflower Compact

B the Articles of Confederation

C the Virginia Statute on Religious Freedom

D the Bill of Rights

30 Which of the following was the *most* important long-term effect of the U.S. purchase of Alaska?

F increased space for a growing U.S. population

G increased agricultural land

H access to vast natural resources

J access to a large warm-water port

31 All of the following are ways that American citizens actively participate in civic affairs *except*—

A lobbying elected officials to support legislation

B voting in local, state, and federal elections

C watching the news on television

D volunteering time to political caimpaigns

32 In World War II, the term *D Day* referred to—

F the dropping of the atomic bomb

G the battle of Dunkirk

H the Allied invasion of Normandy

J the day that Germany surrendered

33

> **GOALS OF THE NEW DEAL**
>
> 1. Help farmers by raising crop prices and delivering low-cost electricity to farms
> 2. Improve economic conditions in the Tennessee Valley area by developing hydroelectric power
> 3. Guarantee the right to organize and establish a minimum wage
> 4. Provide work for those Americans who were left unemployed by the Great Depression

The Public Works Administration, the Civilian Conservation Corps, and the Works Progress Administration were programs designed to realize—

A Goal 1

B Goal 2

C Goal 3

D Goal 4

Go On

34 One of the advantages that Virginia had over the other colonies was that John Rolfe, an early settler in the colony, planted a crop that generated large amounts of money for its planters. This cash crop was—

F cotton

G corn

H tobacco

J wheat

35 The development of the first atomic bomb was the *primary* result of which of the following?

A the Manhattan Project

B the Marshall Plan

C the invasion of Pearl Harbor

D the election of Harry Truman as president

36 Francis Scott Key wrote "The Star-Spangled Banner" during which of the following wars?

F the French and Indian War

G the American Revolution

H the War of 1812

J the Civil War

37

Major Works of the Muckrakers		
Ray Stannard Baker	*Railroads on Trial*	Abuses of the railroad industry
Frank Norris	*The Octopus*	Farmer's struggle with the railroads
Upton Sinclair	*The Jungle*	Abuses by the meatpacking industry
Ida Tarbell	*History of the Standard Oil Company*	Business practices of monopolies

The muckrakers listed would be *least* interested in examining—

A abuses of corporate power

B unfair labor practices

C separation of church and state

D corporate treatment of immigrants

38

1905	American authorities take over the Dominican Republic's economic policy
1906	American marines occupy Cuba
1909	American marines occupy Nicaragua
1911	American authorities take over Nicaragua's economic policy
1915	American marines occupy Haiti
1916	American authorities take over Haiti's economic policy
1916	American marines occupy the Dominican Republic

The above actions are examples of the American foreign policy that President William Howard Taft dubbed—

F the Open Door policy

G dollar diplomacy

H laissez-faire

J the Monroe Doctrine

39

"The heavy pall of smoke constantly overhangs her ..., [the hills] have been leveled down, cut into, sliced off, and ruthlessly marred and mutilated, until not a trace of their original outlines remains.... [The city exemplifies] all that is unsightly and forbidding in appearance, the original beauties of nature having been ruthlessly sacrificed to utility."

—*Visitor to Pittsburgh, Pennsylvania, in the nineteenth century*

The description above refers to the results of—

A automobile pollution

B overpopulation

C industrial despoliation

D suburban sprawl

40 Which of the following famous Americans associated with the abolitionist movement was an escaped slave?

F Frederick Douglass

G William Lloyd Garrison

H James Birney

J Harriet Beecher Stowe

Go On

41 All of the following provisions were part of the Compromise of 1850 *except*—

A acceptance of California as a free state

B passage of the Fugitive Slave Act

C adjustment of Texas's border

D prohibition of slavery in all lands gained in the Mexican Cession

42 American Indians taught the colonists skills that had a large impact on which of the following aspects of colonial life?

F urbanization

G agriculture

H religion

J music

43 President Woodrow Wilson's vision of an international organization that would bring governments together in an effort to promote world peace is *most* clearly reflected in which of the following organizations?

A the Works Progress Administration

B the North Atlantic Treaty Organization (NATO)

C the United Nations

D the Warsaw Pact (the Warsaw Treaty Organization)

44

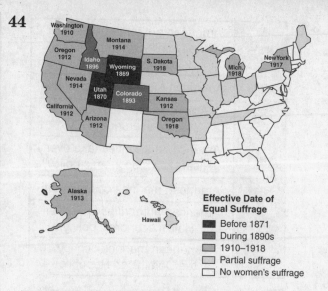

Based on the map above, it would be reasonable to conclude that the greatest opposition to women's suffrage was concentrated in the—

F West

G South

H Northeast

J Midwest

45 The Bay of Pigs invasion, authorized by President John F. Kennedy, was an attempt to unseat which of the following communist leaders?

A Fidel Castro

B Ho Chi Minh

C Kim Il Sung

D Mao Tse-tung

46 In response to the stock market crash of 1929 and the onset of the Great Depression, President Franklin D. Roosevelt proposed legislation to do all of the following *except*—

F create public employment projects

G undertake massive government-sponsored infrastructure projects

H decrease regulation of banks

J increase foreign trade by reciprocally lowering tariffs

47 The *primary* purpose of constructing the Panama Canal was to—

A aid commerce between the United States and South America

B expand U.S. colonial holdings

C showcase U.S. technological advances

D link the Atlantic and Pacific oceans

48 All of the following policies limited slavery in American territories *except*—

F the Proclamation of 1763

G the Northwest Ordinance

H the Missouri Compromise

J the Compromise of 1850

49 The Great Compromise between the large and small states at the Constitutional Convention led directly to which of the following features of the federal government?

A the system of checks and balances

B the vast scope of the judicial branch

C the limited power of the executive branch

D the bicameral legislative branch

50 Which of the following colonial documents was ratified by the Second Continental Congress?

F *Common Sense*

G the Constitution

H the Declaration of Independence

J *The Federalist Papers*

Go On ➡

51 The importance of a limited federal government that Thomas Jefferson and James Madison advocated through the Democratic-Republican Party is *most* clearly echoed in the values of which of these political parties?

A the Democratic Party

B the Liberty Party

C the Know-Nothing Party

D the Republican Party

52 Those colonists who supported a continued relationship with Britain and opposed the patriots were known as—

F Anti-Federalists

G American Indians

H Libertarians

J Tories

53 At the end of World War I, President Woodrow Wilson was disappointed because the United States failed to—

A renew American isolationism

B station American troops in Russia

C expand trade with Germany

D cooperate in the League of Nations

54 All of the following founders were authors of *The Federalist Papers except*—

F Benjamin Franklin

G Alexander Hamilton

H John Jay

J James Madison

55

> I am one of the most famous third-party candidates to run for president. Although I did not win when I ran on the ticket of the Bull Moose Party, I had earlier served as president as a member of the Republican Party.

The words above describe—

A Eugene Debs

B Theodore Roosevelt

C Woodrow Wilson

D Franklin D. Roosevelt

56 The stock market crash of 1929 and the onset of the Great Depression eventually led to which of the following government agendas?

F the Great Society

G the Fair Deal

H the New Deal

J the New Freedom

57 Which of the following technological innovations contributed *most* to the new, fast-paced lifestyle popular in the 1920s?

A the telegraph

B the automobile

C the phonograph

D the train

58 Which of the following twentieth-century Constitutional amendments does *not* directly defend or expand individual rights?

F Nineteenth Amendment, enfranchising women

G Twenty-second Amendment, limiting presidential terms

H Twenty-fourth Amendment, eliminating poll taxes

J Twenty-sixth Amendment, lowering the voting age

59 The Thirteenth Amendment guarantees which of the following?

A voting rights for men over the age of twenty-one

B abolition of slavery

C freedom of speech

D voting rights for women

60 The primary result of the December 7, 1941, Japanese attack on Pearl Harbor was—

F the beginning of the Cold War

G the creation of the atomic bomb

H increased popular support for U.S. entry into World War II

J economic recession in the United States

61 The January 1776 pamphlet written by Thomas Paine that helped solidify support for colonial independence from Britain was—

A the Articles of Confederation

B *Common Sense*

C the Declaration of Independence

D *Letters from a Farmer in Pennsylvania*

Go On ⟹

62 The economic theory implemented by President Ronald Reagan is known as—

F the domino theory

G isolationism

H trickle-down economics

J "trustbusting"

63 The fall of the Berlin Wall and the collapse of the Soviet Union marked the—

A end of the Cold War

B end of the Korean War

C success of the League of Nations

D failure of the Marshall Plan

64 Untenable work conditions imposed by industrial powers led to the expansion of labor unions, which used collective bargaining and work stoppages to fight for better working conditions. Which of these reforms was a result of labor union efforts?

F the Food and Drug Act

G regulation of banks

H the forty-hour work week

J the Works Progress Administration

65

The Domino Theory

The domino theory was a foreign policy that proposed which of the following arguments?

A If a communist revolution were to succeed in one Asian country, then other nearby nations would also turn to communism.

B Foreign policy in Asia was a game.

C If one Asian country were to become a democracy, then other nearby nations would also become democracies.

D If the United States colonized one Asian country, then the Asian trade market would open dramatically.

66

> "I have a dream that one day this nation will rise up and live out the true meaning of its creed: 'We hold these truths to be self-evident that all men are created equal'.... I have a dream that my four little children will one day live in a nation where they will not be judged by the color of their skin but by the content of their character. I have a dream today."

This landmark "I have a dream" Civil Rights speech was delivered at the 1963 March on Washington, D.C., by—

F John F. Kennedy

G Malcolm X

H Martin Luther King Jr.

J Rosa Parks

67

> **PROPOSED CHANGES TO THE SUPREME COURT**
>
> 1. Change the number of justices on the Court
> 2. Limit the Court's appellate jurisdiction
> 3. Imposed voting restrictions on Court decisions
> 4. Permit Congress to override Court decisions

Franklin D. Roosevelt's failed plan to "pack" the Supreme Court falls under the category of—

A Proposal 1

B Proposal 2

C Proposal 3

D Proposal 4

68 Which of the following pieces of legislation was a response to muckraking?

F the Federal Reserve Act (1913)

G the National Industrial Recovery Act (1933)

H the Immigration Act (1924)

J the Pure Food and Drug Act (1906)

69

> People from my country immigrated to the United States during the 1870s and early 1880s. Avoiding the big cities where many earlier immigrants had settled, most of us moved to the Great Plains, motivated by the Homestead Act of 1862. Along with Swedish, our language was the primary one spoken in the Dakotas then.

The speaker of the above words *most* likely came to the United States from—

A Ireland

B Norway

C England

D Mexico

70 Increased industrialization had which of the following effects on the rural population of the United States?

F The number of skilled workers in rural areas increased.

G Rural populations decreased as many people left farms to find jobs in cities.

H Many people fled to rural areas to escape urban traffic and pollution.

J Rural populations increased as many people left cities for jobs on farms.

STOP

ANSWERS AND
EXPLANATIONS
FOR THE PRACTICE TESTS

ANSWERS AND EXPLANATIONS
FOR PRACTICE TEST 1

1 **B** The Constitution was written to replace the insufficient Articles of Confederation, **A**. The Fourteenth Amendment was one of the Civil War Amendments that the southern states had to ratify as a condition of their rejoining the Union. This means that the Fourteenth Amendment was not ratified until the middle of the nineteenth century. You can therefore eliminate **C**. Once you figure out that the Fourteenth Amendment wasn't written until the nineteenth century, then you can eliminate the Nineteenth Amendment, **D**, because by definition it came even later than the Fourteenth Amendment. The only answer left is the Bill of Rights, **B**.

2 **J** Abraham Lincoln was the first successful candidate of the Republican Party (in 1860). For more on the context of the incorrect answer choices, see "The Big Picture" section at the beginning of this book.

3 **A** The Civil Rights Act of 1964 and the Voting Rights Act of 1965 were major pieces of legislation that came out of the Civil Rights movement. The purpose of these pieces of legislation was to extend Civil Rights to all Americans, regardless of race. Therefore, they were attempts to eradicate racial injustice. The question gives you a big hint by using the Civil Rights Acts of 1964. After all, this bill sounds a great deal like part of the Civil Rights movement, and it did coincide with the later years of the Civil Rights movement. Because the Civil Rights movement was an effort to eradicate racial injustice, it makes sense that the Civil Rights Act would have had similar goals.

4 **F** You can solve this one by eliminating incorrect answer choices. The Iroquois Nation, **G**, was a confederation of American Indian tribes; it was not an organization of colonists. The Tories, **H**, were the colonists who supported maintaining an allegiance to Britain, which is the opposite of what the question is looking for. The Federalists, **D**, were an influential group of colonists who supported the Constitution. But the Federalists were not arguing against the Tories; by the time the Federalists and the Anti-Federalists were sparring over the details of the federal government, the American Revolution was over and independence from Britain was achieved. The only possible answer, therefore, is the Sons of Liberty, **F**, who you should also recognize as the group who sponsored the Boston Tea Party.

5 **D** Of these famous founders, only Alexander Hamilton, **J**, was not from Virginia. Hamilton was from New York.

6 **G** Upon accepting the Democratic Party nomination for president in 1932, Franklin Delano Roosevelt said, "I pledge you—I pledge myself to a new deal for the American people." When he became president, Roosevelt proposed a dizzying number of legislative initiatives to help lift the United States out of

the Great Depression. His entire legislative agenda is known as the New Deal. The terms *Great Depression* and *New Deal* should be permanently linked in your mind when you think of the 1930s. The other answers might all sound familiar because each was a legislative program proposed by other presidents. The Fair Deal, **F**, was Harry Truman's attempt to renew the principles of the New Deal after the end of World War II. The Square Deal, **H**, was the general theme of Theodore Roosevelt's administration, by which he promised to treat both individuals and corporations fairly, thereby giving everyone a "square deal." The Great Society, **J**, was the large-scale social improvement project that Lyndon Johnson proposed in the late 1960s.

7   **D** There are two ways to go about answering this question. In this question the years covered are 1870 through 1910, a time of massive European immigration to the United States. That knowledge alone eliminates all of the answer choices except for the correct one. The graphs themselves, however, are fairly clear, so you could answer this question even if you did not remember the historical context. This question asks you to synthesize information from two different graphs. In general, the graph representing immigration from northern Europe doesn't change much, while the graph representing immigration from eastern Europe shows a marked increase across the forty-year period. Because the increase in eastern European immigrants is so large, it outweighs any minor fluctuations in the first graph. Even without actually adding the numbers together, it should be apparent that the total number of immigrants increased every decade during the period represented.

8   **H** This is a common-sense question. The question does not require you to know which constitutional amendment is which; instead, the answer choices tell you what each amendment says. Thus, this question asks you only to read carefully and to apply some logic in eliminating the answer choices. Although the Fourth Amendment, **F**, and the Twenty-first Amendment, **J**, protect and expand personal liberties, neither of them illustrates the success of the suffrage campaign. The Sixteenth Amendment, **G**, also does not relate to the suffrage campaign. None of these amendments mentions voting, elections, or other facets of suffrage. The Nineteenth Amendment, though, mandates the enfranchisement of women. The Nineteenth Amendment allowed women to vote in elections, the ultimate success of the suffrage movement. **H** must be the answer.

9   **C** This is a common-sense question. The best approach is to eliminate the answer choices by thinking about them critically. It doesn't make sense that Americans are using public transportation more than private cars, **A**, or that the demand for cars in the United States has been decreasing, **B**. Traffic in this country is as bad as it has ever been, and that should prove both **A** and **B** wrong. As for **D**, the number of jobs available in one industry should not

be significantly affected by the number of jobs available in another industry. For example, if there was a national shortage of high school teachers, that wouldn't result in fewer available jobs in the automotive industry. It does make some sense, however, that increased use of computers and robots on assembly lines in automobile plants would displace workers. Because this is the only answer that passes muster on the common-sense test, go with it.

10   **F** Judicial review is the principle that the judiciary branch of the federal government can invalidate laws that the judicial branch deems to be unconstitutional. Judicial review was established by Supreme Court Chief Justice John Marshall's opinion in *Marbury v. Madison* in 1803.

11   **A** Eliminating clearly incorrect answers can help you find the answer to this question. The French and Indian War, **B**, was not an uprising by American Indians against the colonists; it was a war pitting the British and the colonists against the French and American Indians. The Trail of Tears, **D**, was not an uprising; it was a forced relocation of the Cherokee tribes to Oklahoma. That leaves King Philip's War, **A**, and the Stono Uprising, **C**. The Stono Uprising was a slave revolt in South Carolina. King Philip's War was an uprising led by tribal leader Metacom (the colonists called him King Philip) against the colonists on the western frontier of Massachusetts.

12   **G** The author of *The Jungle* is Upton Sinclair, who is perhaps the most famous of the muckrakers. But you do not need to remember that information to answer this question. The question helps you by reminding you that the muckrakers were journalists who wrote about the abuses of industry. That said, the descriptions of the novels give you enough information to indicate whether or not they fit into the muckraking milieu.

13   **D** Your knowledge of the American Revolution should include the major events that led to the colonists declaring independence from Britain. The Navigation Acts, **A**, were trade restrictions and tariffs, as were the Townshend Acts, **C**. The Proclamation of 1763, **B**, was a British order immediately after the French and Indian War that the colonists not move west of the Appalachian Mountains. The 1763 date should give away that it could not have been a response to the Boston Tea Party (which occurred in 1773). The only remaining choice is the Coercive Acts, **D**. The Coercive Acts, also known as the Intolerable Acts, were punitive measures designed to punish the colonists for their activities. Among these measures was the closing of Boston Harbor.

14 **G** You should know that the Articles of Confederation provided for a federal government that was too weak to oversee the entire nation and that the Continental Congress, the only central authority under the Articles, was unable to resolve all disputes among states. The only answer choice that fits is **G**.

15 **A** Many of these questions test your common sense as much as, if not more than, your knowledge of U.S. history. The only inventions that could mitigate the size of New York as an inconvenience would be the ones that made the city smaller (the automobile) or the ones that made communication easier. The automobile is not on the list of choices, and telegraphs were too expensive and inconvenient for widespread local use and already in use before 1867 (the date of Twain's complaint). The telephone it is.

16 **J** The forced journey of slaves from Africa to the New World was called the Middle Passage because it was the middle leg of the journey slave traders took from Europe to Africa to America, then back to Europe. This brutal passage was a journey many Africans did not survive.

17 **C** This question gives you a graph that is not entirely necessary if you know your history. You should know that there is no possible way that unemployment decreased consistently between 1915 and 1942, **A**; this period does include the Great Depression, after all. For the same reasons, you can quickly eliminate **D**. That leaves you to decide between **B** and **C**. Answer choice **B** doesn't really make sense, and a brief look at the graph confirms **C**. After 1933, unemployment generally declined, increasing very slightly from 1939 to 1942, but overall plummeting from the 1933 high of 24.9 percent to the 1942 low of 4.7 percent.

18 **H** The illustration of Columbus's landing in the New World suggests that the first interaction between Europeans and American Indians was a friendly exchange. You can see the two groups standing before each other, with the American Indians offering goods to the explorers. You can easily eliminate **G** and **J** because the image clearly isn't violent. Finally, you can eliminate **F** because the two cultures look strikingly different in their mode of dress.

19 **B** Andrew Jackson pioneered the "spoils system" whereby government appointments are rewarded to supporters who are owed favors. Eliminating incorrect answer choices may be difficult, but you can think about what you know about the presidents to arrive at the correct answer. Jackson was a president who was famously different from his predecessors, both in background and in leadership style. Therefore, he is a good choice.

20   **J** To choose which American Indian tribe the English Jamestown settlers interacted with the most, you have to know approximately where the settlement was located. Jamestown was settled in present-day Virginia, along the middle of the North American coastline. If you know this geography, you can look on the map to find the tribe who lived there, the Powhatan. The other choices list tribes that were either too far north (Mohawk and Wampanoag) or too far south (Timucua).

21   **D** Your knowledge of history should make you familiar with some of the key issues of the contemporary women's movement. One of the key elements of post–World War II feminism was the right to equal employment opportunities.

22   **F** The mid-nineteenth century belief that the United States was destined and obligated to control as much territory in North America as possible was known as manifest destiny. Although it may be difficult in this case to use process of elimination to arrive at the correct answer, there is a clue in the question: the word *destined*. This word is found again in **A**. Manifest destiny caused the United States to push American Indians off their lands and to add territories and states to the Union continually throughout the nineteenth century.

23   **A** All of the men listed in the answer choices are famous colonial rabble-rousers, but your knowledge of the American Revolution should certainly include *Common Sense*, written by Thomas Paine. Patrick Henry, **B**, is a Virginian famously quoted as saying, "Give me liberty or give me death!" Samuel Adams, **C**, was a leader of the Boston Tea Party and a cousin of John Adams. John Jay, **D**, was one of the pseudonymous authors of *The Federalist Papers*.

24   **F** To answer the question you need to consult the map and see which colonies have areas indicated as tobacco producing. You might also bring your historical knowledge into play. Southern states, more than northern ones, relied on tobacco as a cash crop.

25   **C** Use the map to find out what products were shipped from Europe to the American colonies and Africa in the eighteenth century. Arrows pointing from Europe to the other continents are labeled "Manufactures." Because you know that Europe industrialized before the Americas and had a more complex economy with many specialized craftsmen, it makes sense that Europe provided manufactured goods to the rest of the world during this century. You can eliminate tobacco, sugar, rum, meat, and grains, because these are all products that were shipped from the Americas to Europe.

26   **J** The trade triangle illustrated by this diagram shows the continents trading across the Atlantic Ocean in the sixteenth and seventeenth centuries. To choose the correct answer, you have to think about which important trade center belongs in the unlabeled brown box, namely Europe. European shipping companies carried goods across the ocean during this era, spreading Europe's economic system and culture all over the Western hemisphere.

27   **C** Throughout the nineteenth and twentieth centuries, cities in the United States grew. Until the 1920s, the percentage of the population living in rural areas was larger than the percentage of the population living in urban areas, and has continued to dwindle in the decades since. Cities in the United States grew as a result of industrialization, drawing rural Americans to cities for employment. Although foreign immigration, **A**, contributed to the growth of cities, it did not contribute significantly to migration *within* the United States until more recently. And, although reduced soil quality, **D**, is an appealing answer because it sent thousands of Americans from the dust bowl to California, the dust bowl was only a small part of the trend toward urbanization.

28   **J** Your knowledge of the New Deal should allow you to answer the question by eliminating some of the clearly incorrect answers. The New Deal was a series of presidential initiatives, most of which were passed by Congress. The Supreme Court was noteworthy because it struck down quite a few pieces of New Deal legislation. Neither **F** nor **G** is acceptable: The former fails to mention Roosevelt's role in creating the New Deal, and the latter fails to mention the important role Congress played in creating the New Deal. **H** is far too extreme to be the correct answer, even if there is a school of historians who would suggest that the New Deal would have been even more effective had the Supreme Court not deemed some of the legislation unconstitutional. That leaves **J** as the only possibility.

29   **D** Strict construction is the notion that the Constitution should be interpreted very literally, thereby curtailing the power of the federal government. Thomas Jefferson advocated this position for most of his political career. For example, his opposition to the Alien and Sedition Acts led him to help draft and support the Virginia and Kentucky Resolutions, **C**, and to oppose the First National Bank, **B**. Jefferson's authorship of the Virginia Statute on Religious Freedom, **A**, does not relate to the Constitution. The only possible answer is the Louisiana Purchase, **D**. The purchase of new lands and the creation of new territories was an exercise in federal authority that was not clearly provided for in the Constitution; it was, therefore, a departure from Jefferson's usual approach.

30   **G** Your understanding of World War I should include tanks, airplanes, submarines, dirigibles (blimps), machine guns, and poison gas. All of these were relatively new inventions that changed the face of war. *Nuclear* submarines, however, were not invented until after World War II.

31 **C** This is a common-sense question. Most people don't have a "Causes of the Dust Bowl" list at the tips of their tongues, so you need to use the answer choices to help you find the right answer. **A** is a fairly obvious cause of the dust bowl. **B**, while less obvious, seems to make sense: The removal of vegetation, by overgrazing and overplanting, eliminated the natural system for holding the soil in place. **C** does not make much sense at all. How would people leaving their farms cause the dust bowl? In addition, your knowledge of the Great Depression should tell you that people left their farms *because* of the dust bowl, not before it. **D** does make sense. Although you may not know whether or not farmers overproduced during World War I, it would make sense that treating the land poorly would eventually lead to damaged land that yielded poor crops. **C** is correct.

32 **G** Common sense strikes again. The Eisenhower interstate system was the proper name of the network of highways crisscrossing the United States. Although it is true that these highways were built with the added consideration that they could serve as emergency landing strips for planes, they are primarily intended for automobile travel (and, of course, trucks).

33 **B** You can find the right answer to this question by eliminating incorrect answer choices. Only one of the battles in the answer choices took place in the Pacific theater of World War II. The Battle of San Juan Hill, **C**, was a famous battle involving Theodore Roosevelt and the Rough Riders in the Spanish-American War. The Battle of New Orleans, **D**, was fought in the War of 1812. The invasion of Normandy, **A**, on D Day was a decisive moment in World War II, but it took place on the European front against the Germans and the Italians. The Battle of Midway was the turning point of World War II in the Pacific because it was the first decisive American victory against the Japanese. After a string of clear Japanese victories following the bombing of Pearl Harbor and the American declaration of war, the United States halted a Japanese offensive in the battle of the Coral Sea. But the Battle of Midway was the first successful American offensive against the Japanese, and it turned the tide in World War II.

34 **J** Common sense dictates that the answer must be either the telegraph or the telephone. The question gives you three clues: the name Alexander Graham Bell, the year 1876, and the phrase *business and personal communications*. Even if you do not remember that Alexander Graham Bell invented the telephone, you might know that the telegraph was in use before 1876 or that the telegraph was not widely used for personal communications.

35   **C** Use your knowledge of history to eliminate the incorrect answers. The Monroe Doctrine, **A**, was a foreign policy position adopted by President James Monroe. The Monroe Doctrine focuses on limiting European influence in the Western hemisphere and has little to do with the conflict between the federal government and states over states' rights. Eliminate **A**. As president, Thomas Jefferson approved the Louisiana Purchase (which was negotiated by James Madison), and it seems unlikely that he would oppose westward expansion, so you can eliminate **D**. Thomas Jefferson did oppose the creation of the First Bank of the United States, **B**, but the bank was not the subject of the Virginia and Kentucky Resolutions. The Virginia and Kentucky Resolutions were written in response to the Alien and Sedition Acts, **C**, both of which expanded the federal government's power to regulate immigration and limit the freedom of speech. Both Madison and Jefferson felt these acts gave too much power to the federal government and upset the balance of power between the federal and state governments.

36   **J** Again, use your knowledge of history to eliminate the incorrect answers. The United States bought Florida in 1819. Britain's, **G**, only claims in North America by that time were in Canada. France, **F**, sold its possessions in North America to the United States under the Louisiana Purchase in 1803. Mexico, **H**, did not become a participant in American negotiations until the annexation of Texas was discussed in the late 1830s (although it wasn't completed until 1845).

37   **B** It makes no real difference that the quote provided is from U.S. Senator Orville Platt. You are not expected to know anything about Senator Platt, nor are you expected to have ever heard of Senator Platt. The best approach to this question is to eliminate all the answers that do not make sense. The only answer that actually makes sense is **B**. Although there is some appeal to **C**, the idea of colonial expansion is not in conflict with isolationism. If the United States were to follow Senator Platt's advice and abandon isolationism, then the United States would have to engage other nations in some kind of interaction. Only economic interaction—trade—makes sense.

38   **G** U.S. military forces fought in the Korean War to enforce the U.S. policy of containment. Containment was based on the theory that the United States had to confront the spread of communism at every opportunity. Détente was a policy of greater cooperation and enlarged trade with communist nations; it was a Nixon policy, which means that it was introduced almost twenty years after the Korean War. Even if you were unsure between **F** and **G**, your understanding of the Cold War should eliminate **H** and **J**, both of which are opposite of what actually occurred.

39 **A** The Battle of New Orleans was the last battle in the War of 1812, **B**, vaulting Andrew Jackson to national fame, **C**, and was fought after the United States and Britain had agreed to the treaty that would end the war, **D**. The only answer choice that isn't true is **A**. The British did try to burn Washington, D.C., during the War of 1812, but it happened before, and therefore not in response to, the Battle of New Orleans.

40 **H** Popular sovereignty was the notion that residents of a territory should determine for themselves the status of slavery in their territory. This idea was put into practice by the Kansas-Nebraska Act, **H**, which led to the events of "Bleeding Kansas." Each of the three other answer choices deal with slavery, but none approach it from the angle of popular sovereignty.

41 **D** The chart provides the population figures for the ten largest cities in the United States in 1870 and again in 1910. During the period in between, the Industrial Revolution really accelerated in the United States. Although some of the cities on the lists were major commercial centers, the growth between 1870 and 1910 was mostly industrial growth. This is indicated by the appearance of industrial centers like Cleveland, Pittsburgh, Detroit, and Buffalo on the 1910 list when they were not on the 1870 list. African American migration north came later in the twentieth century.

42 **G** The Civil War Amendments, added to the Constitution in the aftermath of the Civil War and intended to redress slavery and its related issues, were the Thirteenth, Fourteenth, and Fifteenth Amendments. If the question asked for a condition of Reconstruction, the period following the Civil War, then the answer must be one of the Civil War Amendments. The Thirteenth Amendment outlawed slavery. The Fourteenth Amendment redefined citizenship and guaranteed all citizens equal rights. The Fifteenth Amendment gave all male U.S. citizens over twenty-one years of age the right to vote. Southern states were required to ratify the Fourteenth Amendment as a condition of being readmitted to the Union; without the support of the former confederate states, the Fourteenth Amendment would not have garnered three quarters of the states' votes required for a Constitutional amendment.

43 **C** This is a common-sense question. The growth of Los Angeles and San Francisco necessitated more freshwater in California (as opposed to the undrinkable salt water of the Pacific Ocean). The incidents in the box do not support **A**, because the federal government is not mentioned in the example about Los Angeles. Neither do the events support **B**, because Los Angeles and San Francisco continued to grow. **D** mentions environmental pollution that is not apparent in the information given. **C**, mentioning the tension between urban growth and environmental protection, is the only answer that passes the common-sense test.

44   **F** The United States dropped the atomic bomb on Japan (first on Hiroshima, then on Nagasaki) to end the war in the Pacific theater of World War II. The Berlin Airlift, **G**, was undertaken in response to the Soviet occupation of Berlin after Germany surrendered to end World War II. The North Atlantic Treaty Organization (NATO) **H** is a strategic alliance created to protect western democracies from Soviet aggression during the Cold War. The Truman Doctrine, **J**, was an American policy to provide economic and military assistance to democratic nations fighting against direct and indirect communist aggression. The first exercise of the Truman Doctrine was aid to Greece and Turkey in 1947.

45   **B** You can find the answer by eliminating incorrect answer choices. The American Dream—the primary clue given in the text provided—refers to economic opportunity and the ability to improve one's economic status through hard work and democratic advancement.

46   **H** Even if you don't remember the specific holding of *McCulloch v. Maryland*, you can find the correct answer by eliminating incorrect answer choices. The concept of judicial review, **F**, was actually decided by *Marbury v. Madison*. The requirement that the arrested be read their rights, **J**, was decided by *Miranda v. Arizona* (hence the nickname "Miranda rights" for the list of rights that must be read). And your basic knowledge of the Constitution and the Supreme Court should make you certain that there have been no Supreme Court decisions ruling that states can nullify federal laws as they see fit, **G**. That leaves only federal supremacy, **H**.

47   **B** Your knowledge of the American Revolution and the Constitution should make Thomas Jefferson's famous phrase about "life, liberty, and the pursuit of happiness" recognizable as an excerpt from the Declaration of Independence.

48   **G** The Civil Rights movement was an effort to eradicate racial injustice. **H** might help eradicate racial injustice if it were true, but the Ku Klux Klan still exists. The poll tax, **G**, the practice of charging a tax for access to the ballot box, was a significant hindrance to many African Americans trying to exercise their rights to vote. The Twenty-fourth Amendment was a significant step toward providing full Civil Rights to African Americans. The election of John F. Kennedy, **F**, while arguably helpful to the Civil Rights movement, was not an accomplishment of the movement. The Twenty-sixth Amendment, **J**, which was not ratified until the 1970s, was not a response to the Civil Rights movement as much as to the Vietnam War.

49   **D** This is another common-sense question. Although **A**, **B**, and **C** may be sound reasons to build the Panama Canal, **D** simply does not pass the common-sense test. Even if the United States hoped to profit from the operation of the Panama Canal, the construction itself was extremely expensive and difficult.

50   **J** This is a bit of a trick question. The Fifteenth Amendment, **G**, enfranchised African American men over the age of twenty-one, but the poll taxes implemented by many states and localities prevented the majority of African Americans from voting for almost another one hundred years. The Civil Rights Act of 1964, **H**, helped desegregate public accommodations and accomplished other important advances to end Jim Crow, but it did not increase the number of African Americans able to vote. The Voting Rights Act of 1965, **J**, however, was passed in response to the difficulties that Freedom Summer volunteers had in registering African Americans to vote in the South. This bill was the beginning of substantive progress to allow more African Americans to vote. It was followed by passage of the Twenty-forth Amendment, which outlawed poll taxes.

51   **A** Perhaps the greatest contribution that George Washington made as president was setting good precedents. Despite public pressure to continue as president, Washington chose to step down after two terms because he feared that to serve longer would undermine the foundations of democracy that the Constitution established. No president served more than two terms until Franklin D. Roosevelt sought and won a third term in 1940. In the 1950s, the Twenty-second Amendment was added to the Constitution, officially limiting the presidency to two terms.

52   **H** Freedom summer, **F**, the founding of the Southern Christian Leadership Conference (SCLC), **B**, and the Montgomery, Alabama, bus boycott, **J**, were all events of the Civil Rights movement. The Seneca Falls Convention was a major event in the women's suffrage movement. If you were unsure about this one, you might know that Seneca Falls is in the North, while most of the major events of the Civil Rights movement took place in the South.

53   **D** There are five clues in this question, even though it seems like there is very little information given. The question tells you that you need an immigrant (that alone eliminates Thomas Edison, who was born in the United States, and Marconi, who never immigrated to the United States). You also need a scientist, which all of the people listed were. The question then gives you three accomplishments. The Manhattan Project, which was the development of the first atomic bomb during World War II, suggests a date in the 1940s. The confusing part is that all of the names are likely familiar. Edison invented the phonograph and the incandescent lightbulb, among many other creations. Marconi and Tesla each claim to have invented the radio, although the credit usually goes to Marconi, despite evidence that Tesla created a working radio first. Einstein is often cited as the most important scientist of the twentieth century; he contributed to the creation of the first atomic bomb (and later spoke often on the need for world peace), and he revolutionized the study of physics with his theories on time, light, space, and relativity. He is most famous for the equation $E = mc^2$.

54 **F** The Nullification Crisis was an 1832 showdown between South Carolina and the federal government over the national tariff. Although the issue of slavery, **J**, is a tempting answer choice (as it frequently led to states' rights conflicts between states—often led by South Carolina—and the federal government), slavery was not the primary issue South Carolina was fighting in 1832.

55 **C** Neither Patrick Henry, **A**, nor Thomas Jefferson, **B**, participated in the Constitutional Convention. Henry was an ardent Anti-Federalist, and Jefferson was serving as ambassador to France. George Washington, **D**, served as chair for the Constitutional Convention, but he did not have a leading role in the actual drafting of the Constitution. James Madison, **C**, not only wrote most of the Constitution, but also presented and advocated for the Virginia Plan and the system of checks and balances, which combined to lay the groundwork for most of the Constitution.

56 **H** During World War II, while many young American men went to fight, there were widely expanded opportunities for women to work. This fact should be part of your store of knowledge about World War II.

57 **C** The proliferation of automobiles has enhanced numerous industries, from the construction of roads to the manufacture of steel, rubber, and other car parts. Using common sense, you should find that the only possible answer is petroleum processing, the industry that produces the gasoline that cars need to run.

58 **H** The crash of the stock market on Black Tuesday was the beginning of the Great Depression. The Great Depression was therefore a result of Black Tuesday, not a cause of it. The same is true of **F** and **G**—unemployment and bank failures, respectively—which were also results of the stock market crash.

59 **C** In the early years of World War II, the United States was hesitant to get involved. The turning point was the Japanese bombing of Pearl Harbor in Hawaii. The surprise attack on Pearl Harbor led to greater public support for American entry into the war, which allowed President Franklin Roosevelt to ask Congress for a declaration of war. The German invasion of the Sudatenland in Czechoslovakia, **A**, was one cause of the European outbreak of World War II, but it was not an immediate cause for American involvement. The Cuban missile crisis, **B**, was an event of the Cold War and happened after World War II. The assasination of Archduke Ferdinand, **D**, was not a cause of American entry into World War II. It was the cause of World War I.

60 **G** The earliest settlers in Massachusetts, both the Pilgrims and the Puritans, came to North America to escape religious persecution. They were persecuted because they criticized the Church of England as corrupt. They came, therefore, seeking the freedom to practice religion as they saw fit.

61 **B** W. E. B. Du Bois wrote *The Souls of Black Folk*. Susan B. Anthony, **A**, was a leader of the women's suffrage movement. Martin Luther King Jr., **C**, and Rosa Parks, **D**, were both important figures from the Civil Rights movement, which largely occurred in the 1950s and 1960s. The question's hint that the book was published in 1903 therefore helps eliminate these answer choices.

62 **G** This is a common-sense question, but it could confuse you if you think too deeply about it. The test expects you to make your decision based upon the information given, which, in this case, is a chart showing increasing oil consumption. Which of the answer choices would not be a solution to the environmental problems caused by increased oil use? **F**, **H**, and **J** would all be effective solutions. However, **G**, using coal, would not improve environmental conditions.

63 **D** The first slaves arrived in North America in 1619. At that time, of the choices given, Virginia was the only established colony.

64 **F** Coming in the years after the War of 1812, the Monroe Doctrine, **F**, was the United States' declaration that European nations were no longer welcome to interfere in affairs of the Americas. The Tariff of Abominations, **G**, was the tariff on imported goods imposed during the 1820s. The Good Neighbor policy, **H**, and the Open Door policy, **J**, both came much later. The Good Neighbor policy did prescribe U.S. relations with Central and South America, but it did not involve Europe. The Open Door policy was issued in regard to China.

65 **B** Think about a suburb. It's a residential community outside of a city, and most of the residents usually commute into the city for work. The commute was made possible by the popularization of personal transportation (automobiles), as opposed to mass transit.

66 **H** Eliminate answers you know to be incorrect and you can answer this question even if you have forgotten the details of the War Powers Resolution. The information given about the War Powers Resolution says nothing about the Supreme Court, so eliminate **J**. The resolution was passed in 1973, during the Vietnam War, which makes **G**—that U.S. military forces were not being used often enough—very unlikely. "The Big Picture" about the Vietnam War includes the fact that the presidents—from Kennedy to Johnson to Nixon—never asked for a congressional declaration of war. The resolution came from the Congress, making it unlikely that the resolution would criticize Congress (this assumption can be concluded from the information included in the box as well). The only possibility is **H**.

67 **A** Again, eliminating incorrect answers is a good way to approach this question. The information provided does not mention regulation of business, **B**. In addition, the programs expanded the size of the federal government, eliminating **C**. Even if the expansion of the government is not apparent from the information given, this outcome should be part of your understanding of the Great Society. There isn't a direct relationship between the Great Society and the New Deal, so you can eliminate **D**. Both were programs that expanded the size and scope of the government, but the New Deal was largely an *economic* policy initiative, while the Great Society was largely a *social* policy initiative.

68 **G** Gerald Ford became president when Richard Nixon resigned. Nixon chose to resign rather than face impeachment over the Watergate burglary and the subsequent cover-up, collectively known as Watergate. Even if you did not remember that history, the date should help you eliminate **H** and **J**, both of which occurred earlier in the century. The Vietnam War did not end until 1975, and when it did, the president did not refer to it as a nightmare; the United States withdrew from Vietnam with as much honor and pride as was possible given the situation. Thus, the only possible answer is **G**.

69 **A** Answer choice **B** is simply too extreme to be the answer, not to mention that it fails the common-sense test. New York is not on the map, so there is no way that the answer could be **C**. **D** is not supported by the map, which does not include rivers. The only possibility is **A**.

70 **J** For the most part, President Woodrow Wilson's famous Fourteen Points for how the world should proceed after World War I were uncontroversial among the victorious Allied powers and were thus implemented. There was great dissent in the United States, however, over Wilson's final recommendation—the establishment of the League of Nations. The U.S. Senate, fearing a loss of sovereign American power, refused to join the League of Nations, much to the dismay of Woodrow Wilson. After World War II, however, the United States did join the League of Nations' successor, the United Nations. The refusal of the United States to join the League of Nations (which was the brainchild of President Woodrow Wilson) should be a major component of your knowledge of World War I.

ANSWERS AND EXPLANATIONS FOR PRACTICE TEST 2

1 **A** The Jamestown colony, founded by the British in 1607, eventually succeeded because of help from the Powhatan Confederacy of American Indians (specifically, its leader, Powhatan) and because of the decision to grow and export tobacco. Jamestown was not in an exceedingly warm climate, and the European settlers there did not import African slaves until after the colony had proven successful. Rather, instructions from American Indians about what food to grow and how to grow it helped them to survive. Additionally, the cash crop tobacco became popular in England and was a profitable export.

2 **G** The pamphlet suggests that some Europeans tried to understand the language of the American Indians. It shows the efforts of one Englishman to put down the rules of the Indians' language into a form Europeans could understand. This effort suggests that the two widely different groups of people did try to understand and communicate with each other, even adopting each other's words.

3 **C** The migration of American Indian tribes to the west of the Mississippi River during the Jacksonian Era was due in large part to the Indian Removal Act of 1830. This question can be answered without the help of the map, but the map does help you to visualize the migration and think about why so many different tribes would all move. You can eliminate **B** because it would be highly unlikely that all of that land would have been overfarmed. Likewise, the map helps you to eliminate **D**, the Mexican-American War, because you can see that Mexico isn't close to the land being evacuated. Finally, **A**, the Taft-Hartley Act, can be eliminated because this piece of legislation was passed more than one hundred years after the Jacksonian Era.

4 **F** Federal banking policies changed under President Andrew Jackson's leadership when he dissolved the Second National Bank. Jackson didn't like the existence of a federal bank because he thought it benefited only rich New Englanders. His fight against the bank was popular with voters as well. Jackson vetoed the bill that would have renewed the bank's charter and then appointed a friend to the position of secretary of the treasury to withdraw funds from the bank. Given these facts, you can easily eliminate **G** and **J**, which speak to the establishment of federal banks. Likewise, **H** can be eliminated because the government did not take a bigger role in regulating the economy during this era.

5 **B** When you answer this question, keep in mind that the time period you are being asked about is the late 1800s. In the late 1800s, industrialists began to expand their businesses by buying related companies and forming trusts. The correct answer choice is **B** because this action made corporations larger and stronger, which fueled faster economic growth.

6   **J** Slavery in the United States reshaped the lives of African families trapped in this institution by breaking up families as members were sold to different owners. Because slave owners thought of Africans as property, not people, little effort was made to keep parents with their children or husbands with their wives. **F** can be eliminated because you know that most African American children were not educated during the era of slavery. Likewise, **G** and **H** can be eliminated because African Americans and whites were not integrated and slavery did not encourage strong African family units in the United States.

7   **C** Abolition was a key political issue in the first half of the nineteenth century. The poem in question was written to convince citizens to support abolition initiatives to end slavery. This intention is made clear by the graphic description of the brutal conditions slaves faced. Furthermore, the poem refers to slaves who are sold and separated from their families as "stolen." People who supported the continuation of slavery downplayed the harsh conditions in which slaves lived and did not think of slaves removed from their families as stolen. You can eliminate **D**. Although the poem does mention women—the "stolen daughters," slavery is the key issue. You can eliminate **A** and **B**, which regard women's suffrage.

8   **F** The Missouri Compromise dealt with the divisive slavery issue as new states entered the Union by preserving the balance of slave states and free states. It also set a boundary north of which slavery would be banned. The map helps you to see the outcome of the compromise by marking this boundary. It is easy to eliminate **J** because you know that the United States never had two federal capitals. You can also eliminate **G**, because no date was set for the abolition of slavery, as well as **H**, because it doesn't speak to the boundary that was created as a result of the compromise.

9   **D** The Supreme Court ruling *McCulloch v. Maryland* asserted the supremacy of federal law over state law, helping to clarify the role of states in the Union. This question is tough because eliminating answers is difficult unless you know a little something about each of the cases given as choices. It is a good idea to review the five or six major Supreme Court cases before you take the exam.

10 **F** Jamestown was the first successful colony in Virginia.

11 **A** Although Henry Ford is most widely known for inventing the automobile, his invention of the assembly line is arguably equally important. Common sense indicates that Ford did not invent the steam engine, **B**, which allowed for the expansion of the railroad before the Civil War. Even though Ford famously doubled his workers' wages, it seems unlikely that he conceived of the forty-hour work week, **D**, which was a major victory of the labor movement. Because railroads were already widely used before Ford entered the business world, it does not make sense that he would have invented the railroad engine, **C**.

12   **J** This question does not require the cartoon if you remember your World War I history. The Treaty of Versailles was the official end of World War I between the Allied powers and Germany (other Axis countries had to sign other treaties). The treaty was a harsh, punitive document that decimated Germany's military power and embarrassed Germany and its citizens. The only answer choice that fits the historical facts is **J**. The cartoon does help if you are unsure. The tall, upright men represent the countries that negotiated the Treaty of Versailles (Britain, France, Italy, and the United States), while Germany is clutching the treaty and looking small, abashed, and glum. This basic picture eliminates **G** and **H**. The fact that Russia does not appear in the cartoon at all eliminates **F**.

13   **A** This is a common-sense question. Common sense tells you that automobiles allowed people to spread out a little bit. That eliminates **B** and **D**. Your understanding of post–World War II history should include the fact that the United States was becoming increasingly urban during the twentieth century. This fact allows you to eliminate **C**. The only answer left is **A**.

14   **H** Your knowledge of the Civil War must include an understanding of the relative strengths and weaknesses of the Union and the Confederacy. Most important, you need to understand that the Industrial Revolution had transformed the North into a manufacturing economy, but had not done so in the South. As a result, the Confederate States of America lacked the industrial infrastructure, the railroad network, and the factories that they needed to win the Civil War.

15   **B** Elizabeth Cady Stanton, Susan B. Anthony, and Lucretia Mott were all driving forces behind the women's suffrage movement, which culminated with the Nineteenth Amendment, giving women the right to vote. The fact that all of the people named in the question are women is a major hint to steer you toward **B**, the only answer that is a movement that was exclusively for the benefit of women.

16   **F** The first two settlements in Massachusetts were Plymouth and the Massachusetts Bay Colony. Of those, only Plymouth is among the answer choices. Your knowledge of the Pilgrims should include this basic information.

17   **D** The Civil Rights movement did use the courts, **A**, the Congress, **B**, and nonviolent direct action, **C**, to achieve its ends. At no time, however, even after the beginnings of the Black Power movement, did the Civil Rights movement achieve any of its goals through armed insurrection, **D**.

18   **G** The Nullification Crisis pitted President Andrew Jackson against South Carolina in 1832, because South Carolina felt that the high national tariff, **G**, helped the industrial North and hurt the agrarian South. Although the slave trade, **J**, is a tempting answer, it was not the cause of this event.

19   **C** This is another question that asks you about a cartoon, but can be answered without the cartoon. Although the American empire in the Pacific did expand following the Spanish-American War, the Spanish-American War began not because of a dispute about Guam, but because of disagreements about Cuba, **B**. In addition, most of the American colonies in the Pacific had not been Japanese possessions, **D**, and there was little support in Congress for the idea that all of the possessions would becomes states, **A**. Guam, for example, is still an American possession but not a state.

20   **F** The conquistadors—Spanish explorers early in the Age of Discovery—had three primary motivations: to discover legendary deposits of gold in the New World, to convert the American Indians to Catholicism, and to earn fame by accomplishing these goals and discovering new lands to claim on behalf of Spain. These goals are often summarized as "gold, God, and glory."

21   **D** The only way to answer this question is to use both of the graphs. The information on the graphs does not have a clear connection to **B**, so you can eliminate it. If you compare the graphs, there are budget surpluses (in 1880, 1900, and 1910), as well as budget deficits (in 1870 and 1890); that information allows you to eliminate **A** and **C**. **D** is definitely true because the exports grew from $500 million in 1870 to $2,125 million in 1910, a difference of $1,625 million. Imports, on the other hand, grew only $1,500 million (from $550 million in 1870 to $2,150 million in 1910).

22   **H** The Cherokee tribes were forced by the U.S. Army to walk from North Carolina to Oklahoma in the late 1830s. Known as the Trail of Tears, this forced march took place after Martin Van Buren became president. The French and Indian War, **F**, took place in the 1750s, and the Stono Uprising, **J**, was a slave revolt in the late 1730s. You can eliminate these answer choices because they both took place before the American Revolution. You can eliminate the Seminole War, **G**, because it was one of the Indian Wars that made Andrew Jackson famous before he entered politics.

23   **A** Knowing the correct answer to this question requires an understanding of the Red Scare. The role Senator Joseph McCarthy played in the congressional hearings on the supposed communist infiltration of the government and other sectors of American life should be part of your store of knowledge about the Cold War era of American history. The McCarthy hearings were a major event of the 1950s. Richard Nixon was a member of the senate at that time and would be elected vice president under General Dwight D. Eisenhower in 1952. Henry Cabot Lodge was a U.S. senator around the turn of the twentieth century; his son, Henry Cabot Lodge Jr., was Nixon's running mate in the 1960 presidential election.

24 **F** Your knowledge of the 1950s should include the Warren Court, which decided all of the cases in the answer choices. You might recognize *Brown v. Board of Education of Topeka, Kansas*, **F**, and *Miranda v. Arizona*, **J**. *Miranda* was a criminal law case (responsible for "Miranda rights," which start with the phrase, "You have the right to remain silent . . ."), and therefore was not directly responsible for abetting the goals of the Civil Rights movement. *Brown v. Board of Education*, on the other hand, was the most important Supreme Court decision ever for Civil Rights.

25 **C** Containment was the primary American foreign policy goal of the Cold War. Your knowledge of the Cold War should include the Berlin Airlift, **A**, the Cuban missile crisis, **B**, and the Vietnam War, **D**. The only answer left is **C**, the Persian Gulf War, which took place around the same time the Cold War was ending and had nothing to do with communism.

26 **F** The major communications breakthroughs of the nineteenth century were the telegraph and the telephone. Only the telegraph is among the answer choices. Another major development in nineteenth-century communications was the laying of telegraphic cable under the Atlantic Ocean, which made instant communication between the United States and Europe possible for the first time.

27 **D** Be careful here. If you completely ignore the graph, then you might not know which to choose among **A**, **B**, and **D**, all of which are likely true. According to the graph, the population density of the United States increased continually between 1880 and 1940. The question includes the information that the land area of the United States changed very little during the same period of time. For there to be significantly more people in each square mile of the country without the country changing size, the population must have grown. The only answer actually supported by the graph is **D**.

28 **J** Your understanding of the Cold War should include the concept of détente, which involved taking diplomatic action to lessen tensions. The Berlin Airlift, **F**, the Cuban missile crisis, **G**, and the Korean War, **H**, all are examples of containment. In addition, the hint of Richard Nixon in **J** helps, because détente was a policy pioneered by his administration.

29 **B** If the correct answer is not immediately apparent, try eliminating the choices you think are incorrect. The Mayflower Compact, **A**, was the first document in America to outline the separation of church and state. The Virginia Statute on Religious Freedom, **C**, was the first law passed in the United States to make the separation of church and state part of the governmental structure. The Bill of Rights, **D**, followed the example of the Virginia Statute. The Articles of Confederation, **B**, must be the answer.

30 **H** Common sense will help you eliminate all of the answers other than **H**. Alaska is not a state with a large population or a large agricultural industry; these facts eliminate **F** and **G**. By no stretch of the imagination does Alaska have any warm-water ports, so you can eliminate **J**. But it is true that Alaska has a dizzying array of natural resources.

31 **C** It is definitely the case that civic participation includes lobbying elected officials, **A**, voting in elections, **B**, and volunteering for political campaigns, **D**. The only answer left is **C**.

32 **H** The Allied invasion of Normandy, which was the turning point in the European front of World War II, is commonly called D Day. All of the other answer choices are events from World War II, but none bears any relation to D Day.

33 **D** The New Deal included an alphabet soup of programs and initiatives to help pull the United States out of the Great Depression. The PWA (Public Works Administration), CCC (Civilian Conservation Corps), and WPA (Works Progress Administration) were all employment programs designed to provide jobs for the unemployed. That the word *works* appears in two of the program titles is the best clue.

34 **H** Tobacco was the primary cash crop of the colonies in the seventeenth century. Cotton, **F**, was the primary cash crop of the South later on in the eighteenth century, but not until after the beginning of westward expansion.

35 **A** Your knowledge of World War II should include the development of the atomic bomb, accomplished with the help of immigrant scientists—most notably Albert Einstein and Enrico Fermi—in Los Alamos, New Mexico. Their work was code-named the Manhattan Project. The Marshall Plan, **B**, was the postwar foreign policy by which the United States gave money to help European nations rebuild.

36 **H** Francis Scott Key wrote "The Star-Spangled Banner" during a battle at Fort McHenry in Baltimore Harbor during the War of 1812. You can eliminate the French and Indian War, **A**, because it preceded the American Revolution. That leaves you to choose between the American Revolution, **B**, the Civil War, **D**, and the War of 1812, **H**. Your store of knowledge about the War of 1812 should include the composition of "The Star-Spangled Banner."

37 **C** The muckrakers were journalists who worked to expose the abuses of corporate power. Some of their work led to major reforms and regulations. All of the choices are traditional concerns of the muckrakers except **C**.

38 **G** Dollar diplomacy was President Taft's policy of encouraging American industries to invest in Caribbean and Latin American countries. Then, when political or economic problems arose in those countries, the United States intervened to protect American interests. The Open Door policy was part of American policy toward China. The Monroe Doctrine related to other nations in the Western hemisphere (including the Dominican Republic, Haiti, Cuba, and Nicaragua), but it was issued during James Monroe's presidency in the early nineteenth century. Laissez-faire is a general economic theory calling for no government regulation or interference in the economy.

39 **C** The fact that the quote is from the nineteenth century automatically eliminates **A** and **D**, both of which were problems of the twentieth century. The decision between **B** and **C** can be made in two ways: First, Pittsburgh was an industrial city built entirely around the steel industry; second, the description mentions nothing of overpopulated people, high-rise apartment buildings, or fields full of shacks. The quote is entirely about the results of industrialization, and therefore the answer must be **C**.

40 **F** Only one of the people listed in the answer choices was an African American. Frederick Douglass was definitely a slave; he wrote a famous book about his life in and his escape from slavery. William Lloyd Garrison, **G**, was the most famous of the abolitionist leaders, but he was not a former slave himself. James Birney, **H**, was the presidential candidate of the short-lived Liberty party; had he been an African American, he could not have run for office in the years before the Civil War. Harriet Beecher Stowe, **J**, was a novelist (she wrote *Uncle Tom's Cabin*) and the daughter of a prominent Boston preacher. Even if you do not know a great deal about most of the answer choices, your knowledge of the Civil War should include enough information to know Frederick Douglass wrote the most famous slave narrative of all time.

41 **D** The Compromise of 1850 included six provisions, and it's difficult to remember them all. Instead, evaluate each answer choice on the likelihood that it was part of the Compromise of 1850. The first three answer choices should seem like they may have been part of the Compromise (you should know that the Fugitive Slave Act passed as part of the Compromise of 1850). The last answer choice, however, could not have possibly been included in the Compromise of 1850, because it was the subject of the Wilmot Proviso, the platform of the Free-Soil Party, and a contentious issue for many years after 1850.

42 **G** You will often be asked to evaluate the influence that the colonists had on the American Indians; it is less often that you will be expected to do the opposite. This is a question with which common sense can help you a great deal. By the time urbanization, **F**, was an issue, most of the American Indian tribes had been devastated by conflict with European Americans or pushed west onto reservations. The American Indians did not spread their religion, **H**, or their music, **J**, to the colonists in any significant or widespread way. The only possible answer is that the American Indians helped the colonists learn to farm in ways that met the demands of the new land and the new climate. This information should sound familiar from your elementary school lessons on the purpose of celebrating Thanksgiving.

43 **C** You should remember that, after World War I, President Woodrow Wilson proposed Fourteen Points and that the most important of his points was to form the League of Nations. The Senate balked at this proposal, and the United States refused to join the League of Nations. After World War II, however, the United States did join its successor, the United Nations, **C**. The Warsaw Pact, **D**, was a Soviet alliance that counterbalanced the North American Treaty Organization, **B**. The Works Progress Administration, **A**, was one of the many organizations set up by New Deal legislature.

44 **G** This question requires the use of the map provided. The map clearly shows that no state in the South had enacted women's suffrage before 1919. Although many states in the North had not yet enacted suffrage, the North was not as unanimous in its opposition as the South was. As a result, the answer has to be **G**.

45 **A** Your knowledge of the Cold War should include the fact that the Bay of Pigs invasion was an attempt to overthrow the government of Cuba. Even if you do not remember the name of the communist leader of Cuba (in which case you need to watch the news and read the newspaper more often), common sense tells you that it probably wasn't one of the Asian names listed in **B**, **C**, and **D**.

46 **H** The answer choice that does not fit here is **H**, which is actually the exact opposite of what the New Deal legislation attempted to do. To prevent bank failures, the New Deal created new regulations on banks, as well as regulatory programs like the FDIC (Federal Deposit Insurance Corporation). In general, the New Deal was a time of expanding government and greater regulation. The only answer choice that does not fit into that basic view is **H**.

47　**D** The Panama Canal was desirable for numerous reasons, but the primary reason was to allow easier travel and commerce between the Atlantic and Pacific oceans, and therefore the East and West coasts of the United States. The ill will that the Panama Canal created between the United States and some Central American governments made it unlikely that its construction would aid U.S. trade with South American or Central American countries. In addition, although the United States did colonize the Canal Zone for almost the entire century, the Panama Canal was not built for the purpose of extending the American empire. Similarly, although the construction of the Panama Canal utilized American technology, it was not the purpose of building the canal.

48　**F** You should remember that the Northwest Ordinance, **G**, the Missouri Compromise, **H**, and the Compromise of 1850, **J**, all limited the expansion of slavery. But if you are unsure about those answer choices, remember that there was no American territory when the Proclamation of 1763, **F**, was issued; all of the territory still belonged to the British.

49　**D** The Great Compromise was the agreement that a bicameral legislature could meet the desires of large states to be represented proportionally based upon their populations and the desires of small states to be represented equally as members of the United States. The system of checks and balances, **A**, was actually a feature of James Madison's Virginia Plan. The scope of the judiciary's power, **B**, was not decided at the Constitutional Convention; it was a byproduct of John Marshall's later institution of judicial review. The extent of the executive's power, **C**, is still debatable, and certainly was not a feature of the Great Compromise.

50　**H** The Second Continental Congress met before the beginning of the American Revolution, which means that neither the Constitution, **G**, nor *The Federalist Papers*, **J**, was even a consideration yet. *Common Sense*, **F**, was a pamphlet designed to incite the public; it was not a government document, and it was related to the Second Continental Congress in that it helped provide momentum for Congress's decision to commission and ratify the Declaration of Independence, **H**.

51　**D** The notions of strict construction and limited federal government that Thomas Jefferson and James Madison advocated in their Democratic-Republican Party were not lost when the party splintered after the "corrupt bargain" that decided the election of 1824. You can eliminate the Know-Nothing Party, **C**, which was concerned only with blocking immigration, and the Liberty Party, **B**, which was concerned only with slavery. The Democratic Party, **A**, follows the tradition of Andrew Jackson, who significantly strengthened the presidency. The Republican Party, **D**, is known for advocating a limited federal government.

52 **J** In the years before the American Revolution, there was continuous debate between the patriots, who sought independence from Great Britain, and the Tories, who wanted to maintain British rule, albeit with some adjustments. Common sense eliminates American Indians, **G**, and Libertarians, **H**. The Anti-Federalists, **F**, were not an organized group until after the American Revolution, and then they incorporated individuals who had been on both sides of the independence debate.

53 **D** The question asks you what President Woodrow Wilson wanted, rather than what actually happened. That means that the American retreat into isolationism, **A**, is not the answer, despite the fact that it is what happened. Of the other three choices, the only one you know Wilson supported was the League of Nations, **D**. Although Wilson was generally opposed to the draconian treatment of Germany under the Treaty of Versailles, it might be a stretch to say that he wanted to expand trade with the Germans, **C**. **B** is irrelevant and can be eliminated.

54 **F** You should quickly eliminate James Madison, **J**, and Alexander Hamilton, **G**, who definitely were authors of *The Federalist Papers*. John Jay, **H**, is not as memorable, although he did collaborate with Madison and Hamilton on this project. Further confusing matters is the issue that Benjamin Franklin, **F**, is famous for being a writer. He did not, however, participate in the writing of *The Federalist Papers*. You might figure that because Franklin is so famous that had he helped write *The Federalist Papers*, you would likely know that.

55 **B** The most successful third-party candidate ever (even more successful that Ross Perot in 1992) was Theodore Roosevelt, who had already served as president under the banner of the Republican Party. In 1912, Roosevelt ran for election as a member of the Bull Moose Party, pulling a great deal of the Republican vote away from the Republican candidate and resulting in the election of Democrat Woodrow Wilson.

56 **H** Any knowledge of the Great Depression must include the election of President Franklin D. Roosevelt and the implementation of his New Deal. The other answer choices are all government programs, but none was in response to the Great Depression. The Great Society was President Lyndon Johnson's domestic agenda to rid the United States of social problems stemming from poverty, lack of opportunity, and insufficient education. The Fair Deal was President Harry Truman's effort to revive the New Deal after World War II. The New Freedom was President Woodrow Wilson's economic agenda.

57 **B** The image of the 1920s, an era of great social change, includes the popularization of the automobile. No other innovation was as important to changing the lifestyle of that decade as the personal freedom created by the wide distribution of the car.

58 **G** Of all the answer choices, the only amendment that did not directly expand individual rights is the Twenty-second Amendment, which limits the number of terms a president can serve to two.

59 **B** Remember that women's suffrage was accomplished by the Nineteenth Amendment, so you can eliminate **D**. The lowering of the voting age was accomplished by the Twenty-sixth Amendment, which means you can eliminate **A**. Freedom of speech is a fundamental American freedom, defined by the most famous constitutional amendment, the First. All of the answers have been eliminated except for **B**, the abolition of slavery.

60 **H** The Cold War had nothing to do with Japan, so eliminate **A**. Although the atomic bomb was eventually used to end the war with Japan, it was not developed as a direct response to the bombing of Pearl Harbor, so there should be a better answer than **G**. World War II was the real end of the Great Depression, which means that **J** is definitely wrong. It is true that after the attack on Pearl Harbor, American public opinion changed dramatically to favor U.S. involvement in the war. **H** is the best answer.

61 **B** The question gives you two clues. The first, January 1776, allows you to eliminate the Articles of Confederation, **A**, and the Declaration of Independence, **C**, both of which were written later. The second, Thomas Paine, allows you to zero in on *Common Sense*, **B**. *Letters from a Farmer in Pennsylvania* was a pro-independence pamphlet, but it was not written by Thomas Paine and was written before *Common Sense*.

62 **H** Even if you do not know anything about President Ronald Reagan (if, for example, your history class did not get that far in the textbook, which is common), you can answer this question by eliminating answer choices that cannot possibly be right. Eliminate every answer that you know means something other than what you are asked. The domino theory, **F**, is a Cold War foreign policy term. Isolationism, **G**, was an economic policy undertaken after World War I. "Trustbusting," **J**, was an economic policy before World War I, during the Progressive Era. The only answer remaining is trickle-down economics, **H**.

63 **A** The fall of the Berlin Wall and the disintegration of the Soviet Union occurred at the end of the 1980s and the beginning of the 1990s. That timing suggests that those events must have marked the end of the Cold War.

64 **H** The forty-hour work week was implemented as part of the New Deal, but unlike the cases of the regulation of banks and the creation of the WPA, labor unions exerted a great deal of pressure to support the implementation of a forty-hour work week.

65 **A** The domino theory, one of the prevailing foreign policy theories of the Cold War, held that every successful communist revolution would lead to further communist revolutions. In the early decades of the Cold War, the domino theory was mostly used in discussions of Asia; in later decades of the Cold War those concerns shifted to Central America. The best explanation of the domino theory is **A**. The cartoon can help because the hammer and sickle—the symbol of the Soviet Union and a representation of the extension of communism—is on each domino. The only answer choice that mentions communism is **A**.

66 **H** The "I have a dream" speech, among the most famous speeches in American history, was delivered by Martin Luther King Jr. The March on Washington was a major event of the Civil Rights movement.

67 **A** Roosevelt was upset that so many New Deal programs had been declared unconstitutional by the Supreme Court that he proposed increasing the number of justices on the Court to allow him to appoint judges friendly to his agenda. This effort was one of Roosevelt's most notorious failures, as Congress, which was generally friendly to his ideas, overwhelmingly rejected his plan to "pack" the court.

68 **J** The muckrakers were active around the turn of the nineteenth century, which means that all of the answer choices except for **J** came too late. In addition, the apparent subjects of the laws also suggest that **J** is the most likely answer, given that the muckrakers worked on corporate abuses.

69 **B** Use the information in the text to help you eliminate incorrect answer choices. Mexican immigration to the United States is a largely recent phenomenon, **D**, and Irish immigration peaked earlier in the nineteenth century, during the Irish potato famine, **A**. After the American Revolution, there was no pronounced wave of immigration from England to the United States, **C**. The Great Plains region does have a strong Scandinavian heritage, largely deriving from immigrants from Sweden and Norway.

70 **G** Industrialization is the period from 1880 to 1920. Your store of knowledge about this time period should include the fact that people began migrating to cities in order to obtain industrialized jobs. **H** and **J** are inaccurate. **F** refers to skilled workers, those people who have been trained in some sort of trade. Trades were prevalent in cities, but not in rural areas. The only answer choice that does not get eliminated is **G**.

APPENDIX
VIRGINIA AND UNITED STATES HISTORY STANDARDS

Below you will find all the Virginia and U.S. history standards tested by the Virginia SOL: EOC Virginia and United States History test. You do not need to memorize this list but you might find it helpful for review.

Virginia and United States History SOL VUS.2
"THE STUDENT WILL DESCRIBE HOW EARLY EUROPEAN EXPLORATION AND COLONIZATION RESULTED IN CULTURAL INTERACTIONS AMONG EUROPEANS, AFRICANS, AND AMERICAN INDIANS (FIRST AMERICANS)."

Virginia and United States History SOL VUS.4 *b,c*
"THE STUDENT WILL DEMONSTRATE KNOWLEDGE OF EVENTS AND ISSUES OF THE REVOLUTIONARY PERIOD BY
- DESCRIBING THE POLITICAL DIFFERENCES AMONG THE COLONISTS CONCERNING SEPARATION FROM BRITAIN;
- ANALYZING REASONS FOR COLONIAL VICTORY IN THE REVOLUTIONARY WAR."

Virginia and United States History SOL VUS.5 *c*
"THE STUDENT WILL DEMONSTRATE KNOWLEDGE OF THE ISSUES INVOLVED IN THE CREATION AND RATIFICATION OF THE CONSTITUTION OF THE UNITED STATES AND HOW THE PRINCIPLES OF LIMITED GOVERNMENT, CONSENT OF THE GOVERNED, AND THE SOCIAL CONTRACT ARE EMBODIED IN IT BY DESCRIBING THE CONFLICT OVER RATIFICATION, INCLUDING THE BILL OF RIGHTS AND THE ARGUMENTS OF THE FEDERALISTS AND ANTI-FEDERALISTS."

Virginia and United States History SOL VUS.6 *b*
"THE STUDENT WILL DEMONSTRATE KNOWLEDGE OF THE MAJOR EVENTS DURING THE FIRST HALF OF THE NINETEENTH CENTURY BY DESCRIBING THE KEY FEATURES OF THE JACKSONIAN ERA, WITH EMPHASIS ON FEDERAL BANKING POLICIES."

Virginia and United States History SOL VUS.7 *a,b,c*

"THE STUDENT WILL DEMONSTRATE KNOWLEDGE OF THE CIVIL WAR AND RECONSTRUCTION ERA AND ITS IMPORTANCE AS A MAJOR TURNING POINT IN AMERICAN HISTORY BY

- IDENTIFYING THE MAJOR EVENTS AND THE ROLES OF KEY LEADERS OF THE CIVIL WAR ERA, WITH EMPHASIS ON ABRAHAM LINCOLN, ULYSSES S. GRANT, ROBERT E. LEE, AND FREDERICK DOUGLASS;
- ANALYZING THE SIGNIFICANCE OF THE EMANCIPATION PROCLAMATION AND THE PRINCIPLES OUTLINED IN LINCOLN'S GETTYSBURG ADDRESS;
- EXAMINING THE POLITICAL, ECONOMIC, AND SOCIAL IMPACT OF THE WAR AND RECONSTRUCTION, INCLUDING THE ADOPTION OF THE 13TH, 14TH, AND 15TH AMENDMENTS TO THE CONSTITUTION OF THE UNITED STATES."

Virginia and United States History SOL VUS.8 *a,c,d*

"THE STUDENT WILL DEMONSTRATE KNOWLEDGE OF HOW THE NATION GREW AND CHANGED FROM THE END OF RECONSTRUCTION THROUGH THE EARLY TWENTIETH CENTURY BY

- EXPLAINING THE RELATIONSHIP AMONG TERRITORIAL EXPANSION, WESTWARD MOVEMENT OF THE POPULATION, NEW IMMIGRATION, GROWTH OF CITIES, AND THE ADMISSION OF NEW STATES TO THE UNION;
- ANALYZING PREJUDICE AND DISCRIMINATION DURING THIS TIME PERIOD, WITH EMPHASIS ON "JIM CROW" AND THE RESPONSES OF BOOKER T. WASHINGTON AND W. E. B. DU BOIS;
- IDENTIFYING THE IMPACT OF THE PROGRESSIVE MOVEMENT, INCLUDING CHILD LABOR AND ANTITRUST LAWS, THE RISE OF LABOR UNIONS, AND THE SUCCESS OF THE WOMEN'S SUFFRAGE MOVEMENT."

Virginia and United States History SOL VUS.9 *b*

"THE STUDENT WILL DEMONSTRATE KNOWLEDGE OF THE EMERGING ROLE OF THE UNITED STATES IN WORLD AFFAIRS AND KEY DOMESTIC EVENTS AFTER 1890 BY EVALUATING UNITED STATES INVOLVEMENT IN WORLD WAR I, INCLUDING WILSON'S FOURTEEN POINTS, THE TREATY OF VERSAILLES, AND THE NATIONAL DEBATE OVER TREATY RATIFICATION AND THE LEAGUE OF NATIONS."

Virginia and United States History SOL VUS.10 *a,b,c,d,e*

"THE STUDENT WILL DEMONSTRATE KNOWLEDGE OF WORLD WAR II BY

- IDENTIFYING THE CAUSES AND EVENTS THAT LED TO AMERICAN INVOLVEMENT IN THE WAR, INCLUDING MILITARY ASSISTANCE TO BRITAIN AND THE JAPANESE ATTACK ON PEARL HARBOR;
- DESCRIBING THE MAJOR BATTLES AND TURNING POINTS OF THE WAR IN NORTH AFRICA, EUROPE, AND THE PACIFIC, INCLUDING MIDWAY, STALINGRAD, THE NORMANDY LANDING (D DAY), AND TRUMAN'S DECISION TO USE THE ATOMIC BOMB TO FORCE THE SURRENDER OF JAPAN;
- DESCRIBING THE ROLE OF ALL-MINORITY MILITARY UNITS, INCLUDING THE TUSKEGEE AIRMEN AND NISEI REGIMENTS;
- DESCRIBING THE GENEVA CONVENTIONS AND THE TREATMENT OF PRISONERS OF WAR DURING WORLD WAR II;
- ANALYZING THE HOLOCAUST (HITLER'S "FINAL SOLUTION"), ITS IMPACT ON JEWS AND OTHER GROUPS, AND POSTWAR TRIALS OF WAR CRIMINALS."

Virginia and United States History SOL VUS.11 *a,b,c,d*

"THE STUDENT WILL DEMONSTRATE KNOWLEDGE OF THE EFFECTS OF WORLD WAR II ON THE HOME FRONT BY
- EXPLAINING HOW THE UNITED STATES MOBILIZED ITS ECONOMIC, HUMAN, AND MILITARY RESOURCES;
- DESCRIBING THE CONTRIBUTIONS OF WOMEN AND MINORITIES TO THE WAR EFFORT;
- EXPLAINING THE INTERNMENT OF JAPANESE AMERICANS DURING THE WAR;
- DESCRIBING THE ROLE OF MEDIA AND COMMUNICATIONS IN THE WAR EFFORT."

Virginia and United States History SOL VUS.12 *a,b,c,d*

"THE STUDENT WILL DEMONSTRATE KNOWLEDGE OF UNITED STATES FOREIGN POLICY SINCE WORLD WAR II BY
- DESCRIBING OUTCOMES OF WORLD WAR II, INCLUDING POLITICAL BOUNDARY CHANGES, THE FORMATION OF THE UNITED NATIONS, AND THE MARSHALL PLAN;
- EXPLAINING THE ORIGINS OF THE COLD WAR, AND DESCRIBING THE TRUMAN DOCTRINE AND THE POLICY OF CONTAINMENT OF COMMUNISM, THE AMERICAN ROLE IN WARS IN KOREA AND VIETNAM, AND THE ROLE OF THE NORTH ATLANTIC TREATY ORGANIZATION (NATO) IN EUROPE;
- EXPLAINING THE ROLE OF AMERICA'S MILITARY AND VETERANS IN DEFENDING FREEDOM DURING THE COLD WAR;
- EXPLAINING THE COLLAPSE OF COMMUNISM AND THE END OF THE COLD WAR, INCLUDING THE ROLE OF RONALD REAGAN."

Virginia and United States History SOL VUS.13 *a,b*

"THE STUDENT WILL DEMONSTRATE KNOWLEDGE OF THE CIVIL RIGHTS MOVEMENT OF THE 1950S AND 1960S BY
- IDENTIFYING THE IMPORTANCE OF THE *BROWN V. BOARD OF EDUCATION* DECISION, THE ROLES OF THURGOOD MARSHALL AND OLIVER HILL, AND HOW VIRGINIA RESPONDED;
- DESCRIBING THE IMPORTANCE OF THE NATIONAL ASSOCIATION FOR THE ADVANCEMENT OF COLORED PEOPLE (NAACP), THE 1963 MARCH ON WASHINGTON, THE CIVIL RIGHTS ACT OF 1964, AND THE VOTING RIGHTS ACT OF 1965."

Virginia and United States History SOL VUS.14

"THE STUDENT WILL DEMONSTRATE KNOWLEDGE OF ECONOMIC, SOCIAL, CULTURAL, AND POLITICAL DEVELOPMENTS IN THE CONTEMPORARY UNITED STATES BY

• ANALYZING THE EFFECTS OF INCREASED PARTICIPATION OF WOMEN IN THE LABOR FORCE;
• ANALYZING HOW CHANGING PATTERNS OF IMMIGRATION AFFECT THE DIVERSITY OF THE UNITED STATES POPULATION, THE REASONS NEW IMMIGRANTS CHOOSE TO COME TO THIS COUNTRY, AND THEIR CONTRIBUTIONS TO CONTEMPORARY AMERICA;
• EXPLAINING THE MEDIA INFLUENCE ON CONTEMPORARY AMERICAN CULTURE AND HOW SCIENTIFIC AND TECHNOLOGICAL ADVANCES AFFECT THE WORKPLACE, HEALTH CARE, AND EDUCATION."

Virginia and United States History SOL VUS.3

"THE STUDENT WILL DESCRIBE HOW THE VALUES AND INSTITUTIONS OF EUROPEAN ECONOMIC LIFE TOOK ROOT IN THE COLONIES AND HOW SLAVERY RESHAPED EUROPEAN AND AFRICAN LIFE IN THE AMERICAS."

Virginia and United States History SOL VUS.6 *a,c*

"THE STUDENT WILL DEMONSTRATE KNOWLEDGE OF THE MAJOR EVENTS DURING THE FIRST HALF OF THE NINETEENTH CENTURY BY

• IDENTIFYING THE ECONOMIC, POLITICAL, AND GEOGRAPHIC FACTORS THAT LED TO TERRITORIAL EXPANSION AND ITS IMPACT ON THE AMERICAN INDIANS (FIRST AMERICANS);
• DESCRIBING THE CULTURAL, ECONOMIC, AND POLITICAL ISSUES THAT DIVIDED THE NATION, INCLUDING SLAVERY, THE ABOLITIONIST AND WOMEN'S SUFFRAGE MOVEMENTS, AND THE ROLE OF THE STATES IN THE UNION."

Virginia and United States History SOL VUS.8 *b*

"THE STUDENT WILL DEMONSTRATE KNOWLEDGE OF HOW THE NATION GREW AND CHANGED FROM THE END OF RECONSTRUCTION THROUGH THE EARLY TWENTIETH CENTURY BY DESCRIBING THE TRANSFORMATION OF THE AMERICAN ECONOMY FROM A PRIMARILY AGRARIAN TO A MODERN INDUSTRIAL ECONOMY AND IDENTIFYING MAJOR INVENTIONS THAT IMPROVED LIFE IN THE UNITED STATES."

Virginia and United States History SOL VUS.9 *a,c*

"THE STUDENT WILL DEMONSTRATE KNOWLEDGE OF THE EMERGING ROLE OF THE UNITED STATES IN WORLD AFFAIRS AND KEY DOMESTIC EVENTS AFTER 1890 BY

• EXPLAINING THE CHANGING POLICIES OF THE UNITED STATES TOWARD LATIN AMERICA AND ASIA AND THE GROWING INFLUENCE OF THE UNITED STATES IN FOREIGN MARKETS;
• EXPLAINING THE CAUSES OF THE GREAT DEPRESSION, ITS IMPACT ON THE AMERICAN PEOPLE, AND THE WAYS THE NEW DEAL ADDRESSED IT."

Virginia and United States History SOL VUS.4 and VUS.5

"THE STUDENT WILL DEMONSTRATE KNOWLEDGE OF EVENTS AND ISSUES OF THE REVOLUTIONARY PERIOD BY
- ANALYZING HOW THE POLITICAL IDEAS OF JOHN LOCKE AND THOSE EXPRESSED IN *COMMON SENSE* HELPED SHAPE THE DECLARATION OF INDEPENDENCE."

THE LESSON IS ALSO BASED ON STANDARD VUS.5: "THE STUDENT WILL DEMONSTRATE KNOWLEDGE OF THE ISSUES INVOLVED IN THE CREATION AND RATIFICATION OF THE UNITED STATES CONSTITUTION AND HOW THE PRINCIPLES OF LIMITED GOVERNMENT, CONSENT OF THE GOVERNED, AND THE SOCIAL CONTRACT ARE EMBODIED IN IT BY
- EXPLAINING THE ORIGINS OF THE CONSTITUTION, INCLUDING THE ARTICLES OF CONFEDERATION;
- IDENTIFYING THE MAJOR COMPROMISES NECESSARY TO PRODUCE THE CONSTITUTION, AND THE ROLES OF JAMES MADISON AND GEORGE WASHINGTON;
- EXAMINING THE SIGNIFICANCE OF THE VIRGINIA DECLARATION OF RIGHTS AND THE VIRGINIA STATUTE FOR RELIGIOUS FREEDOM IN THE FRAMING OF THE BILL OF RIGHTS."

NOTES

NOTES

NOTES

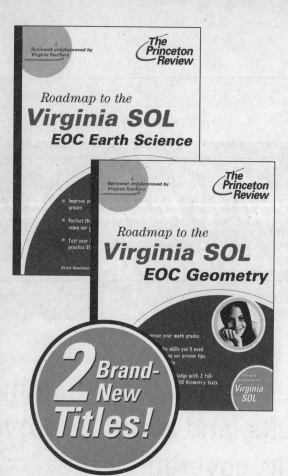